Praise for BIGGER THAN BUSINESS

A must-read for those who seek significance as well as success!

—JACK HERSCHEND, Co-founder, Herschend Family Entertainment

As Christians, we know that God can use our involvement in any profession to help grow His kingdom. The corporate world, however, can make that calling seem especially daunting. Through a series of engaging biographical accounts, Jeff Holler shows us what it looks like to run a business with excellence, integrity, and wise stewardship.

—JIM DALY, President, Focus on the Family

In *Bigger Than Business*, Jeff Holler brings to life the accounts of people who, like me, have been changed by God's power and have applied the truths of His Word to how they operate their businesses. You'll be particularly inspired by how each individual featured in this book fervently seeks the Lord, responds to His direction, and then experiences God's presence to deepen or heal their personal relationships, bless their businesses, and bring great glory to Him.

—NORM MILLER, Chairman, Interstate Battery Systems of America

Jeff brings to life the stories of entrepreneurs around the world that have realized that God can work through them to minister to people through their businesses as effectively as had they become pastors. It is exciting to read the stories of people who are making a difference as stewards of the business with which God entrusted them as they live out the admonition of St. Francis of Assisi: "Preach the Gospel at all times, and when necessary, use words."

—LAWRENCE J. RYBKA, JD, CFP
President and CEO, Second-Generation Owner,
ValMark Financial Group

Bigger Than Business is an outstanding handbook for any Christian business owner or CEO who is truly focused on wanting to build a kingdom-centered company. Each of the chapters is like one facet of a diamond. When read in totality, the reader will have a full understanding of the purpose and underpinnings of a kingdom business.

—**LANE KRAMER**, Founder, The CEO Institute

Through powerful stories of real life people, *Bigger Than Business* raises the right questions and provides thoughtful answers about life, faith, and business. I commend this book to all who want to live richer, more meaningful lives.

—**BILL HIGH**, CEO, National Christian Foundation Heartland,
Author and Speaker

Too few know the stories of saints in the marketplace who have pressed into God's upper story and seen remarkable advances of God's kingdom through business. These biographies will expand the thinking of those who read them and hopefully inspire a grander vision for what God can do in and through a faithful business person!

—**MIKE SHARROW**, President and CEO, The C12 Group, LLC

In a society that urges us to separate our work and spiritual convictions, Jeff provides inspiring examples of those who have refused to check their faith at the office door. I came away encouraged and challenged to not only see business as an opportunity to honor God, but a call to practically and sacrificially trust Him with every dollar and talent He's given me.

—**CHRISTIAN PONDER**, Former National Football League and Florida
State University quarterback

Nothing is more satisfying and liberating for an entrepreneur than having your business be the means to fulfill your biggest purpose in life. Creating such a business, which is unique to each individual, requires vision, self-knowledge, and the right mindset. This book expands thinking on all three of these fronts for those who find their highest purpose in Christ.

—**DAN SULLIVAN**, Founder and President, The Strategic Coach Inc.

In this must-read for families and for the family of believers, Jeff Holler masterfully weaves together the experiences of Christ-following entrepreneurs worldwide to reveal God's all-too-common story; only out of a gratitude to the Savior can true generosity flow. And, because of gratitude, Christ-followers can understand the power of "God owns it all."

—**PAUL WEBER**, President and CEO, Family Policy Alliance

Jeff has done a beautiful job, inviting us into the lives of his friends who are profiled in this awesome guide. When I stop to ponder and write notes while I'm reading a book, I know it's a great one. And when I start sending emails containing excerpts of the book to friends, I know I have found a wonderful learning guide. Well done, Jeff, and thank you.

—**PETER J. KUBASEK**, Founder and Managing Partner, ArkMalibu

The inspiring stories in Jeff's book are a reminder to all of us that entrepreneurship is a divine calling and that, in God's hands, business is one of the kingdom's most powerful instruments of transformation. The world needs more marketplace leaders committed to fulfilling a bigger purpose.

—**J. DALE DAWSON**, Founder and CEO, Bridge2Rwanda

The Lord has shown Jeff the exact stories of *emunah*—faith with action—to illustrate people and their stories of receiving God's instruction and then acting upon it, not knowing the entire process or final result. These stories should inspire many who have the heard the direct call of God to do one particular thing, but who are stuck in neutral because of fear. In today's consultative world, we have too many big visions, expertly-crafted mission statements, and core-value words on posters and websites; what is lacking is the bold action to move from strategy and planning to implementation and the long process of hard work, uncertainty, and release of selfish anchors to fulfill what God's plan is and what He needs you to do in order to accomplish it. These stories should encourage one to let go and start moving!

—**JASON BROWN**, Chief Marketing Officer, Marketplace Chaplains

Jeff Holler's collection of stories implicitly describes the deep loneliness we all face when we are not in proper relationship with Jesus. God created us for relationship with Him and each other in all aspects of our lives. These stories are filled with undeniable affirmation of the efficacy, joy, and peace of bringing our relationship with God to work with us every day.

—**C.W. "DUB" STOCKER, III**, Founder and Former CEO of Lonestar Resources, Inc.

BIGGER
THAN
BUSINESS

REAL-WORLD STORIES OF
BUSINESS OWNERS
LIVING THEIR PURPOSE

JEFF HOLLER

HIGH BRIDGE BOOKS
HOUSTON

Bigger Than Business
by Jeff Holler

Edited by Adam Colwell, Adam Colwell's WriteWorks, LLC

Printed in the United States of America
ISBN (Paperback): 978-1-946615-15-2
ISBN (Hardcover): 978-1-946615-17-6
ISBN (eBook): 978-1-946615-16-9

High Bridge Books titles may be purchased in bulk for educational, business, fundraising, or sales promotional use. For information please contact High Bridge Books via www.HighBridgeBooks.com/contact.

Published in Houston, Texas by High Bridge Books

This book is dedicated to...

My Lord and Savior, Jesus Christ;
my treasured, deeply loved, and loving family; and
to my cherished friends;
all of whom give me purpose and inspire me to remain true to the path
God has prepared for me — wherever it may take me.

It is also dedicated to business men and women around the world who
understand that God created them to serve and glorify Him in the
marketplace, and who relentlessly seek and obediently follow God's will
for them and their businesses.

CONTENTS

FOREWORD

ONE OF THE FOUNDERS of Alliance Defending Freedom (ADF), the ministry I had the honor to lead for more than two decades, was the late Larry Burkett. Millions of Christians over the years benefitted from Larry's teaching on biblical financial stewardship, and I can personally attest to how the application of Larry's principles benefitted not only ADF but my family as well, empowering us to do even more for the kingdom.

One of Larry's key teachings was the principle of the "open hand." The concept was simple. Everything we have comes directly from God. If we realize that all we have is not ours but His, we should hold it with an "open hand" and release those resources as a testimony to the world. When we do so, God can then continue to refill that hand so we can continue to glorify Him. Once we understand this, we no longer live in fear but in contentment, our faith increases, and we are free to give even more.

However, as Larry taught, the opposite is true if we hold everything with a clenched fist. When we hold on to our resources with an iron grip, we are not living any differently than the world. We are saying to God that His provision is ours and not His. The kingdom cannot be expanded, the world is denied the evidence of His grace in our lives, and we live a life that is "all about me." Moreover, with that comes fear, greed, and discontentment because we never have enough to satisfy our desire for more.

This concept goes beyond just finances; it applies to all aspects of our lives, which the following stories attest. When we realize that all aspects of our lives should be held with an "open hand," we become joyful servants sharing the love and grace of God that we have experienced with others, and He is glorified as a result. Whether it is our finances, our marriages, or our communities, the principle of the "open hand" applies.

In the following pages, my good friend Jeff Holler shares the stories of individuals who have learned to live their lives with an "open hand" and how God was able to bring them personal healing and contentment while using their testimonies to bless others. When we realize that everything is His, and we live a life that understands that John 15:5 is true—apart from Christ, we can do nothing—we can truly experience God's love, joy, and peace, and in these fruits of the Spirit, glorify Him to the world. I am confident that these testimonies will be a blessing to you, just as they have been a blessing to me.

ALAN SEARS
Founder, Alliance Defending Freedom
Scottsdale, Arizona

WHY?

THERE WAS ONCE a young, second-generation business owner named Alan who instructed his secretary not to interrupt him because he had a vital appointment. The more experienced chairman of his board came in and said, "I need to see Alan."

The secretary answered, "I'm terribly sorry, but he cannot be disturbed. He's in an important meeting."

Flustered and angry, the chairman stormed past her desk and banged on the door to discover that it wasn't completely closed. It swung open, and the board chairman stopped in his tracks as he saw the young business owner next to his desk—and on his knees in prayer.

Surprised and more than a bit embarrassed, the chairman softly closed the door and returned to the secretary.

"I'm sorry," he said. "Is this usual?"

"Yes," she replied with a smile. "He does that every morning at this time, just like his father did before him."

The chairman of the board responded, "No wonder I come to him for advice."

This story, adapted from Billy Graham's book, *How I Pray*, tells of an executive who had prioritized his spirituality and, more specifically, his relationship with the living God to the point that even an interruption from his board chairman was secondary.

This is a great story, but in today's ultra-demanding business world, how can anyone find the time to pray every day, much less do so at work. And *why* would anyone do so?

I believe the answer solely depends on whether we are committed to following God's plan for our lives, which is exponentially *Bigger Than Business.*

My name is Jeff Holler. I founded and own a company called The Capital Chart Room LTD®, and our firm works almost exclusively with owners of highly successful private companies. I have experienced firsthand many business owners who understand their purpose to be bigger than their business and have witnessed how they are uniquely impacting the world around them.

I decided to travel the world to sit with and interview eight highly respected and successful business owners because I wanted you to get to know them and their stories on an intimate level. Their stories will help you to understand what it means to have a purpose *Bigger Than Business,* and how you can fully live that purpose in and through your business.

These men and women are not the exception. Their stories represent a very small fraction of a worldwide movement of business owners who understand that God created them to serve Him right where they are—at the helm of the business with which He has blessed them. Learning how these men and women have achieved their success while navigating the challenging winds and the waves of the world that buffet them is fascinating, and the business wisdom they share is enlightening. But what drives them—why they do what they do—reveals the heart of their stories.

The eight business owners you will meet in this book are citizens of countries on six continents. With total transparency, they share the good and the difficult sides of their stories.

In the first chapter, you will encounter a U.S. couple who falls to sin and thus incurs personal tragedy. How they experience grace and rise to share what they have learned with others personally and through their business provides a magnificent example for all.

The last chapter is about a merchant with a high school education who built one of the most successful retail businesses in the United States following a time during which he almost lost it all. You will be captivated by how he and his family decided to continue the business through the generations and how they will do so.

In between these chapters, you will learn how, with God's help, a business in Australia that usually serves one client at a time is innovatively leveraged to serve hundreds of thousands around the globe. You will find the subject of this story to be fascinating and inspiring.

You will learn the meaning of *bumpuku* from a Brazilian with a Japanese heritage who, at one point, was fired by his own family, yet ultimately used this experience to come back, as chairman, to help build and continue the family businesses.

In Memphis, Tennessee, you will meet a business owner who, with his co-owner brother, decided to cap their income and give away all the profit that was not reinvested in the company and its employees. You'll be fascinated to discover how and why they then took this concept a step further.

We will travel to Rwanda to introduce you to an amazing woman who barely survived the genocide there and was totally broken yet has gone on to help heal broken hearts and transform lives through the small sewing cooperative she leads.

You will read the incredible story of how a member of an Indonesian family helped their businesses survive the Asian economic crisis, transform, and then thrive over the years, all the while clearing the path for others along the way.

And you will encounter an entrepreneur who was born and raised in communist East Germany as an atheist. He shares his captivating story of how he came to the point today where his heart burns to help other business owners experience the peace and joy derived from a business built and run on biblical principles.

As you read, it may seem that the choices these business owners make and the priorities they establish are out of sync with what the world tells us is normal and correct. I wrote this book, however, because I passionately believe that Christian marketplace leaders around the globe, like this book's subjects, have a unique opportunity to change the world in a fundamental and essential manner. I say "fundamental" because what the book's subjects are doing is at the core of why we were all created; I say "essential" because their stories reveal the key to how humanity was designed by God to live and thrive together.

I promise you will find the subjects of this book, their stories, the business wisdom they share, and their *whys* to be captivating and inspiring. Most importantly, however, I hope that these stories will cause you to contemplate *why* you do what you do. I have included questions at the end of each chapter to help you do so. It is my heartfelt prayer that you will take some time to consider and complete them.

I encourage you, like the young business owner, to petition our Creator each day. Ask Him to help you live the unique and important purpose for which He has created you. As you do, you will be amazed as God leads you forward on the incredible path that He has prepared for you.

After you have read *Bigger Than Business*, I would love to know more about your story and any insights you're willing to share with me.

You can email me at Jeff.Holler@BiggerThanBusiness.com.

AUTHOR'S NOTE

Each story you will read contains three components: 1) the business owner's unique and interesting story, 2) the business wisdom that each person shares, and 3) of course, each subject's *why*. If you don't live in the business world, I encourage you to skim over any of the business wisdom shared that may not be as interesting for you as it will be for those in business. I am confident that you will find the stories and the *whys* that unfold in each chapter to be well worth your time and of significant value to you.

1

RISING FROM ASHES:
RASA FLOORS

Dallas, TX, USA

WHEN THEY MET IN FEBRUARY 1995, Michael and Debbie Rasa were both driven business people raised in very low-income households. They pulled themselves up and out of that type of environment through hard work and determination.

Eight months after founding his company, Rasa Floors, Michael interviewed Debbie for his company's first sales position.

The spark between them was instant because of their shared background, interest, and drive to be successful. She was hired right away.

It started out innocently, but before long, Michael and Debbie found themselves casually flirting and often were in positions that warranted them being away from the other members of the small office for appointments and regular working lunches. Everything was kept professional; they discussed legitimate business issues, but their mutual enjoyment of the times spent together started to become obvious. Soon, office dinners became the norm as they worked late hours together.

Whenever a new client was landed, Michael offered shots of liquor to the employees who were there—all part of the "work hard, play hard" culture he wanted the company to have—and the practice made Michael and Debbie even more relaxed around one another, gradually lowering their inhibitions. Inevitably, the flirting led to more, and that first spark was ignited.

With time, that spark flamed into a sexual relationship. The lies began early with the fleeting feelings of fun and excitement. Living on the edge in work and in play was intoxicating—which they now know were all lies from the pit!

Michael and Debbie fell in love and talk of marriage began. That first introduction, after all, was on Valentine's Day! It was simply meant to be. Right?

But there was a *big* problem—well, two of them. Both were already married to other people, had been so for 12 years, and both had children. When he hired Debbie, Michael and his wife had two daughters, ages seven and eight; Debbie and her husband had a nine-year-old daughter. Michael and Debbie told themselves and each other that they no longer loved or respected their spouses and that their marriages were doomed for failure. They rationalized their choices as their relationship advanced, touch by touch and lie by lie, until they were immersed in an adulterous affair.

They confided with their friends about leaving their spouses and were counseled to be happy and that kids are naturally resilient, so everything would be fine. "The fact that some of our friends were getting divorced at the time," Michael said later, "should have told us something." But they listened to the advice through the filter of their own selfish desires. Michael and Debbie reasoned that they had struggled through their relationships at home and deserved each other too much to let their marriages get in the way of their happiness.

Debbie's divorce was final in 1997—Michael's in 1998. They started dating publicly afterward under the illusion that no one knew about their affair. They were wed on April 3, 1999, and within six months, the two self-professed "type-A control freaks" were fighting almost every breathing moment. Although they loved each other, the flames of their physical and emotional passion had turned on them. Their young marriage was swiftly incinerating into ashes, and the cinders mingled with those left behind from their emotionally burned children and ex-spouses.

Michael and Debbie couldn't help but wonder. *Was there any coming back from this?*

Debbie: The Brokenness of Finding Meaning in Performance

Michael's and Debbie's backgrounds were in some ways similar and in many ways very different. Debbie was born in Des Moines, Iowa in December 1959, the second of four children. Eleven months younger than her older sister and over a year-and-a-half older than her younger brother, Debbie was raised to be self-reliant. She never knew her biological father, and her mother had to work multiple jobs to support the family. Debbie's mother never seemed to have the time, energy, or resources to make an emotionally nurturing connection with her children even though she loved them deeply and protected them fiercely. Because her mother married three times, Debbie grew up assuming people fall in love and get married but get divorced just as easily and move on if things don't work out. When Debbie was eight, her six-year-old cousin was hit by a car and died, an event that prompted her to think more often about the fact that she had never known her biological father.

Debbie also came to believe that she should bury her feelings and just keep working hard and pushing forward. She was often told to "dry it up" because there was no reason to cry. "I was taught to pick myself up by my bootstraps, brush myself off, and plow through difficult situations without dwelling on them or dealing with emotions like fear, anger, or pain," Debbie said.

Still, Debbie was a sweet and kind girl, and a tiny mustard seed of faith was planted in her life starting at age 12. For two years, she and her best friend Kay went together to Sunday school and church. Debbie doesn't recall how she started going to church, but she does remember Mel, her Sunday school teacher who she says was "a wonderful man of God" who,

...in retrospect, was like Jesus in the flesh to me. He made a profound impact on both of us, and when he died shortly thereafter, my faith seemingly died with him.

That same year, Debbie's grandmother, who had also been married three times, took her own life. Debbie was devastated.

In the ninth grade, Debbie met her high school sweetheart who became her first husband three years after she graduated. After only one year of marriage, her husband was imprisoned. "Unbeknownst to me, he was involved in a corrupt business that eventually led to his incarceration," said Debbie. She said it was like a final blow.

I felt like the people I loved ended up leaving me or were taken from me by death. I realize now that I buried a lot of grief and pain because I had no idea how to deal with it. I also learned at an early age that life has no guarantees.

Frightened and alone, Debbie decided to move to Tulsa where her mother lived with her third husband with whom Debbie was close and had affectionately called "Dad" since she was ten years old. She wanted to have a fresh start when her husband was released. Feeling abandoned by her incarcerated husband, Debbie soon found herself working double shifts as a waitress and a bartender. She became obsessed with work, and it quickly became the center of her life.

Fifteen months later, just as her husband was about to be released from prison, Debbie's closest friend in Tulsa, Darlene, committed suicide. "My heart was completely broken. I felt like I couldn't breathe," Debbie said.

My mind seemed to be full of crazy thoughts. Subconsciously, I began to build an impenetrable wall of

protection around my heart and made a vow never
to hurt or feel such unbearable pain again.

Debbie's once sweet spirit and kind heart had been deeply
wounded—and a battle for survival began to wage inside of her.
"I did the best I knew how without God in my life. I was desperately lost but didn't realize how lost."

Debbie had learned from her childhood to suppress feelings
and run from circumstances that she did not want to face. She
had no idea how to deal with the anxiety, anger, and fear that
tormented her, and she ended up running into the arms of another man. He was her first affair, and she believed he was her
ticket away from everything associated with the pain she had
been feeling from losing family and friends and from experiencing a failed marriage. As Debbie drank and partied into the
night, she worked increasingly longer hours to numb her hurt.
Her buried feelings were replaced with the sense of security she
felt from her success on the job. "I thought I had it all figured
out," Debbie said.

I would work my way to success in the world's eyes.
"Performing" would be my savior, my path to happiness. I would start over and start fresh again.

Debbie remarried in 1985 when she was 25, and the couple
moved first to Arlington, Texas and then to nearby Plano. Her
life seemed stable, and three years later, they had their daughter
who was the sweetest blessing to Debbie as she had experienced
challenges with being able to get pregnant. But trouble soon
raised its ugly head again as Debbie's pursuit of performance
turned destructive. She was so driven that she came to believe
the lie that her husband was somehow "less than" her and her
workaholic friends because he was only working a normal 40
hours a week while they were working 60 to 70.

I think, subconsciously and in some distorted way, I thought I was better than him because I was working longer hours. How crazy is that? Tragically, even after my precious baby girl was born, I continued to try and prove myself through my performance. I thought—if I was a workaholic, wife, and super mother and performed each role perfectly—I would finally experience the pinnacle of happiness.

She vowed to be a superstar, the best at whatever she did.

I was on my way to the top, confident that my work ethic would lead me to the fulfillment I desperately desired. What an illusion *that* would prove to be.

That was her mindset—and her state of brokenness—when she met Michael and accepted the sales rep position at Rasa Floors.

Michael: Determined to Become Self Made

Michael's Sicilian father and Irish mother had six children together, two girls followed by four boys. Michael, the second youngest of the boys, was born in 1961. The eight of them lived together in a 1,200-square-foot home in Oakland, New Jersey. His father worked three jobs to support the family, and Michael and his brothers cleared their backyard of trees and bushes to create a huge garden and greenhouses. They sold the vegetables it produced in front of their home and kept whatever was left for meals. Michael's family was poor and never had extra money. Their cars were junkers, and they often used the mechanic's A-frame in their backyard to rebuild them or cannibalize parts from one to keep another running. Any clothes that were purchased or given to the family were for the oldest siblings so they could be handed down to the younger children. Michael never wore a stitch of new clothing as he grew up.

Michael's childhood was anything but carefree. His father was physically and verbally abusive—Michael called him a "rageaholic"—and it was a good thing friends were never allowed to visit because Michael and his siblings feared what they might witness if they were there. Michael and his brothers were required to get up at the crack of dawn to get to work in the garden and greenhouses. His father would call the boys only once to get out of their beds. If they didn't comply, he would flip their beds upside down so they would tumble onto the floor. On those rare occasions when they refused to budge, Michael's father would get a two-by-four and "beat the crap out of us," Michael said, adding that, when they were older, "he would also sabotage our cars, our only escape, if he was angry with us."

At age 11, Michael was determined to be independent and set out to look for work. At Tony's Brothers, the local pizza parlor, they laughed him out of the restaurant. Yet Michael wasn't deterred; he decided to "hire himself" and started working three hours each day cleaning Tony's Brothers' parking lot. The owner, Luigi, eventually relented and offered to pay Michael to scrub the inside floors. From there, he worked his way up to dishwasher, then to food preparer, and eventually to pizza cook.

Michael's late nights at Tony's Brothers made his father's early-morning wakeups that much more irritating. One morning, at the age of 14, Michael refused to get up even after he and his bed were violently flipped over. His father attacked him with the two-by-four and beat him to a bloody pulp. He then threw Michael out of the house and told him he was no longer his son. Shortly afterward, Michael's parents divorced, and were both married to other people within 180 days.

Additionally, his older sister and her family moved out of the area and severed all contact with the family. Michael found out much later that his father had threatened to kill his sister's children and that she and her husband had fled out of fear for their lives.

Michael dropped out of school and survived by working full-time at Antonio's restaurant, which was owned by Luigi's brother, Tony, and located 45 minutes from Michael's home. Antonio's was in Vernon Valley, a winter snow-skiing destination in northern New Jersey. Tony opened his home to Michael and bought a ski pass for him. Michael started snow skiing every day from 8:00 a.m. to noon and then worked at Antonio's from 2:00 p.m. to 2:00 a.m. With nothing to do after work, Michael partied, drank heavily, and used drugs. Most nights, he'd get about three hours of sleep and then return to the ski slopes, often still under the influence of the prior evening's vice of choice. This pattern repeated itself daily, and only Tony and Luigi offered him any type of care or concern.

One morning, Michael woke up in the back seat of his car, still drunk and unsure of how he got there. He realized he was out of control and quickly needed to change the trajectory of his life. Michael called his mother who, by then, was living with her new husband and asked if he could move in with them and his two brothers. She told him they didn't have enough room for him; Michael knew that wasn't true because, unbeknownst to her, he had visited his brothers one day while she was away with her husband.

Angry and sad, Michael hung up the phone in disgust and then called his brother, Paul, who was 10 years his elder. Michael had always admired Paul even though they had no real relationship. He also envied Paul, who was married with two children, owned his own home, drove a cool British Triumph TR6 ragtop sports car, and had a successful career as a pharmacist. Desperate, Michael had nowhere else to go or anyone else to turn to if Paul refused to help.

He held his breath as the phone rang. When Paul answered, Michael told him what was happening, and Paul said, "Where are you right now? I will come get you and you can come live with me and my family!" It was Michael's first experience with a true family, and he had no idea how to relate to Paul, his wife, or their children. He was, however, quickly drawn to the love they shared. He had no idea how he was going to do it, but Michael soon resolved that he wanted to achieve everything his brother had: wife, children, home, car, and career.

As Michael discussed his future with Paul, his brother recommended that he join the Army. Michael obtained his GED (a high school general education development or diploma) and enlisted in the Army's delayed-entry program at the age of 17. He trained as a diesel mechanic as working on cars was his only real acquired skill from his days working on the family junkers in the backyard. When he had completed his training, Michael was sent to a base in South Korea and was later stationed at Fort Hood, Texas. After three years of active duty, he left the Army in 1982 for civilian life where he fulfilled an additional three years of inactive service.

Michael then headed to Dallas in his tired, black Chevrolet Vega to connect with an old friend from Tony's. He worked as a diesel mechanic during the day and at his friend's Italian restaurant at night. Nine months later, he stopped being a mechanic to take a new job sorting mail for the U.S. Postal Service overnights after finishing his work at the restaurant. It didn't take long for Michael to fulfill the first part of his resolution; he married the first woman with whom he went on a date. Within three years, he accomplished two of his other goals: he and his wife had two children and owned a 1,300-square-foot home.

Game Changers

Michael refers to "game changers" in his life, the first of which came when he was working at the post office. While sorting mail, he listened to talk radio and especially liked the show hosted by entrepreneur Bruce Williams. Bruce always asked callers three questions: How old are you? What do you do?

What do you earn? At the time, Michael was earning $13,750 a year, and the majority of the callers were making a lot more. As he started taking note of what different people at different ages were doing for work and how much they were making, Michael concluded that the highest earners were pro athletes, surgeons, partners in large CPA firms, trial attorneys, business owners, and salespeople. His formal education had peaked with a GED, and he had a family to support. Therefore, he concluded there was only one realistic option for him: a career in sales. But he had no idea what he could sell.

Michael soon learned that the grandfather of one of his cousins owned a storm door and window manufacturing business in Dallas that his cousin managed. Michael went to work part-time for them in 1983 as a door-to-door salesman to supplement his income and to learn about sales. He completed his night shift at the post office in the early morning, got a few hours of sleep, and then started knocking on doors to sell his products. He found that he liked sales and started making money almost immediately, selling the windows and doors he purchased at about $35 to customers for $75. He made an additional $50 by personally installing each door.

In 1984, Michael decided to pursue a career in sales and, in the newspaper's classified ads, found an opening for a carpet salesman at ITL (Interiors That Lease) and made the big leap, leaving the post office and its steady paycheck for a commission-only position selling small lots of carpeting to apartment complexes. His supervisors at the post office thought he was crazy to leave his stable job and salary for a commission-based sales career and smugly predicted he would soon come crawling back to be rehired. However, Michael was driven, worked harder and longer than anyone else, and rapidly became the company's leading salesperson. Yet that success didn't stop the company from firing him after five years for being, as Michael said, "I became too difficult to deal with due to my high expectations of service."

Michael went to work for Seagull Floors, a competitor of ITL, in 1989. Again, success came quickly, and he became vice president of sales and a member of the board of directors within 24 months. Michael recognized the company needed to change dramatically to continue to grow profitably, so he went to the owner with a list of 10 changes he thought they should implement to become the best and most successful business in the industry. "They were great ideas," Michael said. "But the owner didn't like any of them. Not even one!"

If he was ever going to start his own business, now was the time. Michael understood and liked the apartment industry. There were many units in the Dallas-Fort Worth metropolitan area, and the area's population was growing rapidly, steadily increasing the number of apartment complexes being built. Michael decided to focus his business' service on replacing the carpet when an individual apartment unit was vacated and being refurbished for the next tenant. This service mandated 24-hour turnaround once an order was received, and that required Michael to enter the business with a substantial amount of new carpet inventory.

With great confidence, Michael went to a local bank to acquire a loan, and when the banker asked for his business plan, Michael promised to return with one even though he had never previously heard the term "business plan." His next stop was the library so he could research how to write a proper business plan. He found a program called Business Plan Pro, but he didn't understand many of the questions. Undaunted, Michael dug in, did his research, and nine months later had singlehandedly put together a detailed 275-page business plan that indicated he needed $350,000 to start his business.

He took his plan and loan request to 24 banks—and was promptly rejected by all of them. He didn't give up, though, and the next bank he approached offered to him a Small Business Association (SBA) government-backed loan, and he was able to obtain a $350,000 36-month-term loan. Michael was thrilled and immediately went to work selling his service, Rasa Floors.

Michael's ability to make the sale was phenomenal, and he established excellent internal processes. However, he built his plans around his customers paying their invoices in 30 to 45 days when, in reality, they were paying in 60 to 90 days. Too much of his cash flow was going in the wrong direction, and the banks were not willing to increase his line of credit. After just six months of opening for business, Rasa Floors was on the verge of going under. Michael knew he needed help fast. His father-in-law agreed to lend him $50,000 if Michael could convince each of his top three suppliers to extend Rasa Floors a $250,000 line of credit. Michael succeeded with the suppliers and secured the loan from his father-in-law. The business continued, but each day was a struggle for survival.

"Game changer" number two came from a combination of two invaluable relationships. As he struggled through the first few months of his business' launch, Michael was introduced to Craig Sutton. Craig had enjoyed a lengthy and successful banking career in Dallas and was working as a self-employed outsourced chief financial officer (CFO) for small businesses that couldn't afford a full-time CFO. Craig knew what a small business needed to do to be successful and had a strong network of colleagues in the banking industry who trusted and respected him. Michael hired him for $1,500 a month, which was a sacrifice at the time, but Michael said hiring Craig was the best investment he ever made in his business.

Craig's first move was to dress up the financing offering to make it more appealing for the banks. He did such a great job that three banks ended up bidding for the funding opportunity, and the necessary operating capital was procured. Concurrently, Craig immediately set to work helping Rasa Floors implement much-needed administrative, financial, and reporting infrastructure. They weren't out of the woods yet, but they had the breathing room and the forward thinking necessary to realize profitable growth.

In 1995, Craig helped Michael anticipate and visualize Rasa Floor's future by outlining three phases of growth.

Phase One (1995-2000) was the *survival and breakout* phase. They put a plan in place to survive and then to break through to annual revenue of $25 million. Craig encouraged Michael to visualize the operations needed to achieve that sum of revenue, and they went to work right away to put that vision into place.

Phase Two (2000-2007) was the *expansion* phase. Rasa Floors needed multiple locations to become the dominant player in its respective markets and to increase annual revenue to $50 million. Craig informed Michael that, to accomplish this phase, Rasa Floors would need to transform into a totally reimagined company with different systems, technology, processes, and management.

Phase Three (2008-present) was the *transformation* phase, during which the company needed to become a professionally managed company and increase annual revenue to $80 million. To do so necessitated sufficient sustained growth in revenue and profitability to attract great talent at the management and executive levels. It also required a substantial reduction in debt, not allowing it to increase beyond the absolute minimum amount necessary for emergency capital reserves. Expansion of the branch locations had to continue as well.

Michael loved the plan and was all in!

The other invaluable relationship was with his brother Paul, on whom Michael leaned heavily for advice from the time he started thinking about his new business. Paul had been exceptionally supportive, and they shared their ideas and dreams with one another. It wasn't coincidental that Paul started his own business nine months after Michael founded Rasa Floors. To thank Paul for his unconditional love and acceptance from the time he took him off the streets, Michael gave his brother 10 percent of Rasa Floors' Limited Liability Company (LLC) ownership at its inception. While the company had no monetary value at the time, Michael's love and appreciation was genuine, and he hoped that someday Paul's share of the company would become valuable.

Paul has been a 100-percent active partner since day one, and he and his wife Karen eventually moved to Dallas so he could increase his contribution to Rasa Floors while continuing to grow his own business in New Jersey. Paul became a member of the founding board of directors—along with Michael, Craig, and Debbie—and remains on the board today.

***

Craig also helped to change the game in another significant manner. Michael and Debbie thought nobody else knew about their affair, but it was obvious to others—especially to Craig. He also knew that, shortly after Michael and Debbie wed, their marriage was in trouble. Michael's frustration and anger became fits of rage, and while he functioned exceptionally well at the business, his deep unhappiness was evident to Craig.

Soon after he joined Rasa Floors as an outsourced consultant, Craig shared his faith with Michael and asked if Michael had a church home.

"No!" Michael responded—and wanted to leave it at that. But Craig carefully persisted and, on occasion, asked if he and Debbie had found a church home.

One day, several months after Michael and Debbie were married, Craig queried yet again. Michael had never had a connection with God, nor did he have an interest in forming one. He was raised in a Catholic family and went to Mass with them but never understood the rituals. Besides, if his parents were representative of religious people, he wanted nothing to do with Catholicism or any another religion. In fact, Michael had decided early in his life that he hated religion. "I don't need God or a church home!" Michael tersely responded to Craig.

"Okay," Craig quietly responded. "But how is your marriage, Michael?"

That, Michael knew, was a disaster. All three of their daughters struggled with sadness and pain after their parents' respective divorces, and it was often apparent they were not happy when they were with Michael and Debbie. One of the daughters took it the hardest in the earlier years of their marriage. Michael said,

> It was not uncommon in the months following my marriage to Deb for her and I, following a heated discussion, to end up in closets on the opposite ends of the house in the fetal position, sobbing our hearts out.

The other two daughters didn't say much at first, but their hurt and distress became apparent over time. At the top of the list of the regrets and shame Michael and Debbie have had to deal with is the suffering their choices inflicted on their children.

Slowly Discovering Truth

By the fall of 1999, Michael and Debbie were willing to do anything to save their marriage. Debbie recalled the kindness, gentleness, and peace her childhood Sunday school teacher seemed to possess, so when Debbie's daughter suggested they visit her father's new church, she thought it was a great idea. Michael reluctantly agreed, recalling Craig's persistent witness.

The church was a huge congregation in Grapevine, Texas. While neither of them had any awareness of anything they were hearing and learning because they were such newcomers to Christianity, Michael especially loved the music and was intrigued by the pastor's message about a biblical approach to living. The pastor preached a series on Christian counseling and how all married couples needed help to navigate successfully the obstacles, challenges, and temptations Satan and the world's systems use to destroy God's ordained institution of marriage. Michael and Debbie decided to give it a try and met with a Christian counselor. In their first session, he conveyed to them that their marriage was only as sick as their unredeemed sin. He explained that God had a plan and a blueprint for their marriage and encouraged them to turn to God and follow His will.

Then, the bomb was dropped. The counselor shared that they needed to confess everything to their ex-spouses and children. "It was the last thing in the world we wanted to do or face," said Michael. "But we knew that what he said was true. Something deep inside compelled Deb and me to come clean." Within the next few months, each met individually with their respective children and ex-spouses. They confessed the sin of their affair and asked for forgiveness. It was the hardest thing either of them had ever done.

The confessions also had their revelations. Debbie's ex revealed that he had been aware of her adultery with Michael and had already forgiven both of them. Their daughter wasn't sure what to do with it, but she was willing to pursue Christian counseling to help her deal with the increasing anxiety around all the changes in her life. She also started attending church with Michael and Debbie.

Meanwhile, Michael's ex was justifiably devastated and upset, and she could not accept her children having a relationship with Debbie. One daughter was stunned and went into a stupor-type state, and the other's anger escalated. Eventually, everyone started receiving counseling: Michael and Debbie together, Michael with his daughters, and Debbie with hers. It seemed that their prior friends had been wrong. The kids weren't okay, and Michael and Debbie weren't happy.

Throughout the next 18 months of counseling and working to save their marriage and their relationships with their children and ex-spouses, Michael was too embarrassed to tell anyone else that he was going to church. He kept his church life in a bubble, totally separated from his business. He and Debbie continued growing the business as they had before in a worldly, unbiblical manner. Their old "work hard, play hard" habits continued, including the shots of liquor whenever a new client was landed.

Yet, despite everything else going on—thanks to Craig's plan—Michael and Debbie were able to lead Rasa Floors through a period of exponential growth from four to 140 employees. The rapid growth, though, placed severe stress on the company's finances. It required the purchases of additional inventory at a much higher rate than their receivables were being collected. Additional personnel and overhead were also necessary to keep up with the growth.

Michael and Debbie were hanging on—but barely.

About the time the company hit 80 employees, the Rasa's pastor was conducting a four-week sermon series on the international best-selling book, *The Prayer of Jabez*. Published in 2000 by Bruce Wilkinson, the book taught on the obscure Bible character Jabez and his prayer found in 1 Chronicles 4:10. It reads,

> Jabez cried out to the God of Israel, "Oh, that you would bless me and enlarge my territory! Let your hand be with me, and keep me from harm so that I will be free from pain." And God granted his request.

The message Michael heard was that God wants you to grow your business as long as your motive is to do it all for the Kingdom of God.

Almost simultaneous with *The Prayer of Jabez* study at church, Lane Kramer, who founded the CEO Institute in Dallas in 1990, reached out to schedule a meeting with Michael after Rasa Floors was recognized for the fourth consecutive year as one of the top 100 fastest growing companies in Dallas. The CEO Institute helps chief executive officers build world-class companies consistent with biblical principles and values, and Lane had been the master of ceremonies at the four black-tie gala events honoring Rasa Floors and the other top companies. When Michael and Lane met, Michael felt moved to share his experience at Fellowship Church and what he discerned from *The Prayer of Jabez* study about building one's business in a manner that honors and glorifies God. Lane invited Michael to join a new peer-to-peer board of Christian CEOs that he was forming for which he had already filled 11 of the 12 board positions. Michael declined, and Lane suggested a lunch with him and two of the new board's CEOs. Michael agreed and enjoyed the lunch so much that he accepted an invitation to attend one of the board meetings as an observer two weeks later.

As he sought to understand what he was observing through Lane and his associates, Pastor Young wrapped up *The Prayer of Jabez* study, and Michael had begun a discipline of reciting the prayer every day for 30 days. He repeated the prayer often throughout the day with complete confidence that God wanted to expand His territory through Michael as His steward in the flooring business. At first, he felt the Austin and San Antonio markets were the perfect areas for expansion in Texas. But Pierre Rouly, a person against whom Michael had competed fiercely for a decade prior to opening Rasa Floors, was a partner in the firm that controlled those markets. Michael feared going head-to-head with Pierre again and decided not to expand.

As the holiday season arrived, the annual company Christmas party—a major undertaking for Michael and Debbie—loomed ahead. Since the inception of the company, they had personally selected and purchased three or four personalized Christmas gifts for every employee and sorted them into each employee's gift bag, including size-specific garments and a handwritten personal note to each person. With over 80 employees now on staff, this was a massive and stressful undertaking, and tensions mounted between the couple. The party was a mere three days away when it was time to individually sort the 250-plus gifts, fill the gift bags, and write all of the notes! As

Debbie tried to convince Michael to take a different approach to simplify the task, yet another argument ensued—this one more heated than usual. Michael went into what was now one of his trademark rages and decided to "show" Debbie by sorting and preparing all the gifts by himself. He loaded everything into his brand new Suburban and raced off toward their lake house, which was located an hour away from their Carrollton home.

As Michael sped down the road, his daily prayer was far from his mind as he was overwhelmed with worry about the outstanding receivables and the company's bills that were going to remain unpaid. Just then, he remembered he had committed to attend the CEO Institute's board meeting with Lane early the next morning. As he raced onward, Michael called Lane and left an exceptionally disrespectful, expletive-laced voicemail message. Michael hung up, and almost immediately, smoke began billowing from under the hood of the new vehicle. By the time Michael stopped and bolted out of the door, the entire passenger compartment was engulfed in flames. Right as he was calling 911, Debbie also tried to call to see where he had gone, and he frantically switched between calls, trying to get emergency help while simultaneously telling Debbie what was happening. The Suburban exploded twice as the vehicle and the gifts it held swiftly burned down to the frame. As Michael watched the surreal scene and pondered his narrow escape, he got a distinct feeling that all of it was a strong and clear message from God.

The following Monday, Michael received an email from Lane. Instead of chastising him for his misguided phone message, Lane reminded Michael that God owned Rasa Floors—not him—and that the Lord had entrusted it to Michael's stewardship. Michael realized he had to do the one thing he had been avoiding: commit everything to God and change his ways.

The first person in whom he confided was Debbie. He read Lane's email to her, and they got down on their knees and prayed to God, asking for forgiveness as they cried together. Michael then decided to join Lane's board for Christian CEOs, and the day after concluding his 30-day recitation of the prayer of Jabez, he attended his first CEO Institute board meeting.

Precisely as the meeting ended, Michael's phone rang. It was Pierre Rouly. He told Michael that his partner wanted to get out of the business, but when he declined the partner's offer to sell, the partner approached a competitor to sell. Pierre shared how he had observed Michael's success and liked the way he conducted his business. He asked if he could work for Michael as Rasa Floors' first sales director and bring all of his business in the Austin and San Antonio markets with him. Michael was stunned. He praised God and proceeded to bring Pierre aboard, the former adversary who remains with the company today as Rasa Floors' executive vice president and director of sales.

Michael and Debbie immediately agreed they needed to seek God on a deeper level, and they decided to join one of Fellowship Church's "home teams"—small groups that meet in the leader's home to study, discuss the Bible, and encourage one another toward spiritual growth. They inquired about joining a group in their suburb of Carrolton, and when they found out there wasn't one, they decided to start one themselves. "We didn't know anything about the Bible," Michael said, "and I couldn't think of a better way to learn than to jump in and make the commitment." They attended leadership training, launched the group, and their spiritual growth and relationship with God was propelled forward to a more intimate level.

Becoming Christ-centered

Not long afterward, Michael and Debbie invited Christ into their softening hearts. They also dedicated their business to God, called the employees together, and confessed to everyone their entire story. They boldly conveyed how they had become new people in Christ who were going to be committed to practicing biblical principles and habits in their business and in their personal lives. They invited the employees to hold them accountable and admitted that they were going to need their help to be good stewards and servant leaders of Rasa Floors. The "shots for all" celebrations went down the drain and were replaced by opening every meeting in prayer.

***

Neither Michael nor Debbie have a college education, but they share a thirst for knowledge. Michael began having the entire company read a business-related or motivational book and then come together every Wednesday to discuss the week's assigned reading. Michael instructed everyone to highlight three things each week that "either blew their skirts up or rolled their socks down!" Each employee was expected to share their highlights and why they were important to them. If there were ideas that everyone agreed should be implemented, they discussed how to do them and integrated them into their operations as soon as possible. Michael and Debbie discovered that this process brought out the best in their employees and showed that their opinions mattered and could make an immediate difference. The couple eventually started including biblically-centered materials like *The Maxwell Leadership Bible* and other faith-based leadership books for review and discussion.

More Game Changers

Michael and Debbie also knew they had to improve their organizational structure and operational efficiency to facilitate their rapid growth and be good stewards. This led to "game changer" number three: the appointment of a formal board of directors and creation of an organizational structure that could stay ahead of the growth. It was implemented as follows.

The board was fully transparent and given the responsibility for all strategic decisions.

A senior management team was formed to ensure the successful operation of the company. It was, and remains today, composed of 12 senior managers, a structure modeled after the 12 disciples of Christ.

Each of Rasa Floors' 11 branches have a branch manager and operations manager to ensure the successful and profitable operation of each location.

Michael, Debbie, and Paul are fully transparent as owners, and Michael and Debbie see the employees as family and share everything with them in detail, both good news and bad. They maintain an open-door policy and honestly answer to the best of their ability any question posed by an employee.

They decided to develop talent and promote from within the company. As a result of this and a highly favorable work environment, employee retention is outstanding, and they have many long-term employees.

Michael and Debbie hire and employ the best person for any given job, whether they have a faith background or not. They focus their hiring decisions on whether or not the candidate is moral, ethical, competent for the job, and diligent. No one is pressured to participate in any faith-based activity, and an employee's view on faith has no influence on their advancement in the company. Michael and Debbie do ensure that their employees know the source of the business' values, beliefs, and habits. They do not force their faith on any employee but simply strive to live it in everything they do—and they are always excited to share their faith when someone asks.

The fourth "game changer" came in 2004 when Debbie shared with Michael that they should start tithing 10 percent of the gross profit of Rasa Floors and become more intentional in their giving.

> It meant that, in addition to our church, we should
> give more to ministries with which God had led us

to be intimately involved and were passionate about.

Michael didn't hesitate and knew Debbie's generosity was based on scriptural teachings. They formed a donor-advised fund and have been giving 10 percent or more of their profit ever since.

In addition, Rasa Floors also employs a male and female chaplain at each of their 11 locations to minister to their employees, customers, and their employees' families and friends. Each chaplain's work is confidential, and most discussions are about life outside of work. The only reporting is when the chaplains submit an accounting each quarter on the number of interaction opportunities they have encountered through Rasa Floors' employees and customers. The chaplains are currently engaging in around 1,700 interaction opportunities each year. They also perform weddings, funerals, and jail and hospital visits. All of their services are also available to employees' relatives at no cost.

In addition, employees are given free subscriptions to RightNow Media @ Work, a faith-based internet library (www.rightnowmediaatwork.org) that provides over 5,000 videos from more than 150 Christian publishers and ministries that offer solid, biblical teaching for every person in the family. The videos offer invaluable teaching covering marriage, parenting, finances, recovery, and more from renowned teachers including Les and Leslie Parrott, Chip Ingram, and Dave Ramsey.

***

In 2006, Rasa Floors became debt free and has been ever since. This gives the company a significant advantage over their competitors whose businesses are heavily leveraged, and it has enabled Rasa Floors to make additional acquisitions with cash reserves and profits. Being debt free also aided the company in remaining profitable and continuing to grow during the deep recession of 2008-2009. Craig Sutton identified several key reasons why Michael and Debbie have been successful in building Rasa Floors from a one-man operation to the highly acclaimed $75 million business it is today. He said,

> Michael listens to his advisors and employees and considers our perspective, which makes him different than many leaders. He may not agree and will be quick to share why. However, he will attentively continue the conversation if you have additional pertinent information or insight.
>
> He is also self-educated and a lifelong student who never stops learning and is always seeking to improve.
>
> In the company, Michael's time is dedicated to what he does best and enjoys most, and he augments himself in other areas with people who are best suited for and will most enjoy the responsibilities. This approach increases everyone's pleasure, passion, and productivity with their work.
>
> He hires great people who appreciate and respect our culture and then gets that right person in the right job for their abilities and personality. As a result, our people tend to thrive in their jobs.
>
> Michael manages resources prudently. He controls expenses but not to the degree that becomes detrimental to delivering high-quality service or losing top-notch people. He is willing to invest wisely in his people, technology, and resources in a manner that will improve both efficiency and quality of service simultaneously.
>
> Everyone trusts Michael because he always does what he says he is going to do when he says he will do it. They know they can depend on him and his word. His word and truth are sacred to Michael.

There has always been a philosophy to have the company focus on what we do best and outsource everything else to companies and people who are better equipped to do the job. Rasa Floors is clear about and focused on who they are as a company and how their time, energy, and resources are best invested toward their target business.

Michael insists that, although a plan may become worthless, the planning process is invaluable. He is fully engaged in the strategic planning process, doesn't skip steps, and is willing to adjust as necessary to keep up with the changing business and technology environment.

He controls and manages risk well. He looks at what is being risked with each decision, including and especially reputational risk. He thoroughly considers whether the benefit outweighs the risk before he makes a decision.

Paying off all of the company's debt was a huge priority for Michael after the company reached a point in 2003 where it was having difficulty making payroll. Michael committed to doing everything possible to manage the company's finances according to biblical principles. Rasa Floors can now self-finance its dynamic growth. This not only saves the company a lot of money, but it also gives us a lot of flexibility to make the right decisions for our short- and long-term future. It also enabled us to increase market share during industry and economic downturns while competitors with high debt loads to service were struggling.

Michael encourages and has achieved a very open board of directors. If after stating our cases we don't all agree, it is Michael's role to make the final decision. He is excellent at weighing all the factors and then making an informed, far-sighted decision. Each board member plays an important role by design. Paul is the analyzer while Michael is able and willing to make a quick decision. I strike a balance between the two. Debbie has the ability to look at things from the customer's viewpoint as a result of her eight years of experience as a multi-family property manager. It is also extremely beneficial to have a woman's perspective. Most importantly, Debbie always insists that we take it to God in prayer and not proceed until we have clarity that, in doing so, we are following God's will.

Overall, it all boils down to Michael's exceptional character. God used the tribulations and challenges Michael experienced throughout his life to shape him into the man of faith and character that he is today. Michael, more than anyone, knows he needs God's help, and he looks to God every day for his strength and direction.

Craig also provided some insight into the culture of Rasa Floors before and after Michael and Debbie dedicated the company to God's care and committed it to operating solely on biblical principles and values.

Michael has always been honest and acted with integrity in his business dealings, but before Michael and Debbie came to faith, the company was run in a worldly manner. The focus was on making money, and how much you made was the indicator of your success. It was also a "work hard, play hard" atmosphere; while seemingly energizing, both were ultimately destructive because of the underlying driving motives. The company was, in many ways, narcissistic.

Once the transformation occurred, while the business did not change, the atmosphere was like night and day. The personality of the company has become one that is humble and driven to serve God and His people. Everyone—employees, contractors, customers, strategic relationships—is treated with respect and dignity. The chaplain service that is provided at no cost to employees and their families and friends is also widely used and appreciated.

The implementation of biblical financial principles has also served the company extremely well. Prior to the paralyzing 2008 economic crisis, we had paid off all of our debt and built significant cash reserves. Doing so enabled us to not only survive but also to continue to remain profitable during very bleak times for our industry. It also allowed us to make some strategic acquisitions. Tithing and being intentional with our giving has also been a blessing for the company and for Michael and Debbie personally. They give well beyond a tithe when you consider all of the personal resources they dedicate to their marriage intervention ministry.

Accepting God's Grace

As Michael and Debbie were transforming Rasa Floors, they were also led to lead a personal ministry that continues today. As the circle of individuals aware of their story expanded, they began receiving personal requests to meet as a duo privately with individuals or couples considering divorce for non-abusive reasons most often related to an ongoing affair. These meetings developed from discussions to interventions.

During the course of this ministry, they have met with hundreds of people throughout the United States to share their story and their faith and then ask them to consider their choices.

When someone mentions that things seem to have worked out for them despite their adulterous decisions, Michael and Debbie are quick to passionately point out,

> If we had known what we know today and had God in our lives, we would not have committed adultery or divorced our spouses. We had no clue of the personal pain, shame, and collateral damage our affair and divorces would cause. And we discovered you have the same issues plus new issues with your new spouse.

Michael added,

> We started the marriage ministry because no one spoke the truth to us. Everyone just told us what we wanted to hear. We share all of the misery and grief we inflicted on ourselves and on our families. We learned the hard way that, if you don't have Christ in the center of your life and marriage, you will most likely expect your spouse, your work, or the person with whom you are having the affair to be your savior … to be the one who makes you happy. Looking to anyone or anything other than Christ for your happiness is a recipe for failure!

He said he and Debbie point people to faith in God, to what the Bible says about the sanctity of marriage, and to professional, faith-based counseling as their primary sources of help. About half of those to whom they speak seek assistance. "The half that doesn't almost always come back to us later."

While Debbie is less animated than her husband, she is still intense in her own way and shares that her and Michael's prior success

...was self-centered and self-serving. We thought it was all about us and that we had achieved the results through our own strength and determination. In the end, our personal and family lives burned to the ground, and I believe our business would have as well because Michael was on a path to self-implode. Had we not learned that every good gift comes from God, including our abilities, and dedicated our lives to Him, we would have never known the peace that we experience now.

Debbie explained that she and Michael

...are no longer filled with fear and worry because we know that no matter what happens, if we open our hearts and seek and follow God's will with the right motives, we will be okay. Michael's stress previously manifested itself in his rage. Now, his peace is manifested in his passion!

She added that Rasa Floors hasn't changed.

We just see it differently and go about running it by a new and better set of principles. It's God's, not ours, and we can trust and take everything to Him with faith. Our transformation can be seen in how we live our lives, in the life of our company, and by those with whom we interact. We let those to whom we minister know that they can have this same joy, peace, and hope in their lives, too.

Debbie reconciles the beauty of the relationship she and Michael enjoy today and a marriage and ministry that was born out of their sin by pointing to Romans 8:28 and its declaration that, in all things, God works for the good of those that love Him and who have been called according to His purpose.

> Once we gave our hearts to Christ and accepted and believed that He died on the cross to pay the price for our sins, and that God raised Him from the dead on the third day so that we could be born again spiritually and have new life in Him, God began to work miracles in our lives. It wasn't automatic or quick, but over time and with professional help, we and our families began to heal and grow. For those that love the Lord, God can take whatever we have done or experienced and use it to His glory if we follow His will.

Michael added,

> There are many passages in the Bible about repenting of our sins and then accepting God's forgiveness and grace and that, by doing so, we can have joy and hope for the future. God's mercy, forgiveness, and grace—when we honestly repent—is so pure and exponentially and unconditionally loving that, for many, it is difficult to believe. But the Bible tells us that God can bring us out of wherever we are and whatever we have done and weave us back together in His glory.

He said he and Debbie have experienced God's grace firsthand.

> God delivered us from our guilt, remorse, hurt, and shame even though we didn't deserve it. It is only by the grace of God that we have, as Deb would say, "risen from the ashes" of our sin to beauty.

Michael and Debbie perform their interventions with great pleasure and passion privately throughout the United States but also at the cost of significant time and monetary expenses.

God continues to bless Rasa Floors as it grows. In 2017, the company's revenues were $78 million, and it was once again profitable. It has expanded from one location in 1994 to 11, which are all located in Texas and Oklahoma. As the company grows, so does its complexity as its average invoice is $600, and it processes and completes thousands of jobs each week. The orders are usually received the day before the carpet needs to be installed, so Rasa Floors must be speedy and efficient.

Michael and Debbie are working on what they consider to be Phase Four, the vision and strategies to develop the next generation of professional and family leadership and an ownership succession plan. They believe this will be the next game changer for the company. Paul's son Brad, who was hired as the Longview branch manager in 1999 when he was 20 years old, is expected to be a key player in the succession of the company from this generation to the next. Brad has worked his way up and through almost every function of Rasa Floors: a carpet technician in San Antonio; a sales representative in Austin; a regional manager over the Longview and Waco branches; an IT technician in the home office in Dallas; the assistant to the director of sales; the chief operating officer; and, as of January 1, 2017, president and chief operating officer of the company.

The light of Christ is truly reflected through how Rasa Floors goes about its business and through the relationship Michael and Debbie have with their employees. The company's mission statement says it all:

- To honor God in all that we do.
- To grow people of passion with integrity.
- To provide extraordinary service to our customers, our employees, and our suppliers, while growing profitably.

It is not surprising that the combination of faith-inspired motives and personal passion has brought prestige to Rasa Floors. Debbie has been recognized as the PacTel Top Sales Rep Producer, finished in the top 10 percent of her class at the Tom Hopkins Bootcamp, and was the winner of The Founders Award by Women of Excellence.

Meanwhile, Michael has received the "Dallas 100" award on multiple occasions, which recognizes the 100 fastest-growing companies in Dallas, and has been featured in articles in *D Magazine* and *Dallas Morning News*. In addition to serving on industry and association boards, Michael has attained numerous award-winning achievements as a professional salesperson in selling carpet services to the apartment industry.

Self-described "learning junkies," Michael and Debbie have received coaching and mentoring from some of the finest sales and business coaches in the country such as Zig Ziglar, Jack Welch, Tom Hopkins, Michael Gerber, Tom Peters, Anthony Robbins, Stephen Covey, John Maxwell, and Darren Hardy. But both Michael and Debbie have transitioned away from motivational and personal development workshops. Michael said,

> After we gave our lives to Christ, we made a big shift away from the motivational and personal-development orientation to spiritually-oriented growth and leadership. We weave what we learn with our personal experience of receiving God's mercy and grace through Jesus Christ. This causes us to challenge our motives constantly so we can remain grounded in and continue to seek God's will for our lives and our ministry.

Michael's and Debbie's commitment to restore faith-inspired unity to their family has also been blessed. All three daughters continued in counseling with their parents after Michael's and Debbie's confessions, have come to faith in Christ, have graduated from college, and are doing well in their professions. The daughters also submitted to biblical principles in their dating relationships. Two are now married and, with their spouses, have deepening relationships with the Lord. Michael said that his relationship with his daughter who was so angry and distraught about the divorce and remarriage is stronger than ever. He stayed in counseling with her even when it required him to fly to Denver every month when she was in college.

Michael and Debbie are grateful to have ongoing, meaningful relationships with their ex-spouses.

Debbie eventually connected emotionally with her mother, and they continue to remain close.

Michael's father died a year after Michael founded Rasa Floors. His father visited a couple of times before he passed but never apologized for his abuse. Still, Michael has forgiven him and sees his mother often though they remain distant in their relationship. Michael continues to pray for his mother.

Perhaps, the most remarkable aspect of Michael's and Debbie's story is not how they fell to self-centered sin but rather how they have accepted God's amazing gifts of mercy, unconditional love, forgiveness, and grace. In doing so, they have risen from the ashes of their remorse, regret, and shame to be reborn and experience new life as they seek and follow God's plan for their lives.

> It has only been through God's gift of mercy and grace through Jesus Christ that we have been able to work our way through the shame and guilt. We've given it all to Him with absolute faith and trust, and as a result, He saved us from a life with no joy, no hope, nothing—only the emptiness of worldly pretense, performance, and self-destruction. We also have clarity that God wants to work through us to

help others learn from our mistakes and not fall prey to the same temptations.

Michael and Debbie continue to engage in marriage counseling to build on what they have learned and to constantly strengthen their marriage. Michael said,

> We realize that Satan will continue to attack us, so to this day, we have boundaries and hedges in our relationship we maintain to protect ourselves and our marriage from falling again. We also speak openly with our employees and others about strongly considering their choices and boundaries. God gave us free will, and our choices dictate everything!

Michael and Debbie Rasa continue to rise from the ashes of their prior lives and sin, and they thrive in the beauty of their shared, ever-deepening relationship with Christ. They now see and love themselves as God sees and loves them: as His beloved children. The flames are brighter and hotter than ever, but now, they burn with passion for Christ. And, instead of destroying, these flames refine, rejuvenate, create, and bring light to others.

Personal Reflection and Group Discussion

1. What have you done to protect your most-treasured personal relationships? How can you protect them to an even greater degree?

2. Michael stated, "For those that love the Lord, God can take whatever we have done or experienced and use it to His glory if we follow His will." How have you experienced this in your life?

3. What temptations are you exposed to at work or otherwise that conflict with biblical truths? How do you eliminate or avoid them?

4. Michael was originally driven by his desire to be rich and Debbie by her desire to achieve happiness through her performance. At the core of your heart, what drives you? Why?

5. Do you have a great team of internal or external advisors around you who can provide objective feedback and help you craft and document plans to grow your business? If not, who could you ask to help you in that endeavor?

6. What other spiritual, business, and personal concepts and practices noted in this chapter stood out to you? How will you integrate them into your life and/or business?

2

TRANSFORMING MINDSETS, IMPROVING LIVES:
PSYCHOLOGY CAFE

Sunshine Coast, Queensland, Australia
Rehetobel, Appenzell AR, Switzerland
St. Albans, Hertfordshire, England

THE NEWS THAT entrepreneur, clinical psychologist, speaker, and author Dr. Robi Sonderegger presented to the Christian Economic Forum in 2017 was certainly sobering—and, for some, shocking.

But perhaps it shouldn't have been all that surprising.

His white paper revealed projections from the World Health Organization that mental disorders will be the second-leading contributor to the global disease burden by 2020—with unipolar major depression already listed as the world's leading cause of disability. Even more, psychiatric illness is ranked worldwide almost as high as cardiovascular and respiratory diseases and has surpassed HIV and all types of cancer.

Dr. Robi says there are many derivations of mental illness. There are the more commonly known, such as addictions to drugs, alcohol, gambling, sex, and pornography, as well as anxiety, depression, despair, and bipolar disorder. Then, there are those not as frequently discussed like post-traumatic stress disorders suffered by survivors of war trauma and refugees. Many have experienced this, including strife-torn areas of the Middle

East and Africa—and children who have escaped captivity as a sex slave or child soldier. Add in the myriad of relationship, marriage, child-rearing, and sexual identity issues that can affect a person's thinking, and the depth and breadth of the mental health problem becomes staggering.

Dr. Robi reported that various forms of depression alone affect more than 120 million people globally each year. In turn, this mental instability contributes to intergenerational poverty, homelessness, abuse, neglect, and discrimination. In many places, the mentally ill are marginalized and even excluded from society. He also wrote that the negative economic impact of mental illness on individuals, communities, and even companies is significant. Reduced workplace productivity caused by mental disorders has had far-reaching financial repercussions on businesses worldwide.

Yet Dr. Robi did not submit his findings to the Christian Economic Forum to trumpet a tale of woe and hopelessness. He is convinced that innovative collaboration among the many global leaders that champion God's economic and servant principles can not only address the mental health crisis but begin to stem the problem. He has also championed the Family Challenge Charitable Trust, a mental health charity that provides trauma rehabilitation training around the world, and a variety of other creative initiatives that are addressing the mental health crisis head on.

Dr. Robi is in a unique position of international influence. It's interesting, considering that this man of three nationalities— once best known as a celebrity snowboard instructor for Prince Charles and his son Prince Harry—is now living out his passion to go where no one has gone before to address global mental health care needs. However, a most unlikely series of events and influences saw him crisscross the globe and helped shape who he is today.

Role Model

Dr. Robi was born in 1973, the youngest of two children, in England. He cites his father, Fritz, as one of his greatest influences. Fritz came from a prestigious family in Switzerland. His grandfather, Rudolf, was the Swiss president during World War II (When Adolf Hitler threatened to invade, he stood up to the Fuhrer and essentially conveyed, "Bring it on!"). Fritz's father, Hans, was one of the wealthiest men of the Appenzeller region in Switzerland. Dr. Robi said his father's childhood was not unlike being in the von Trapp family from *The Sound of Music.*

Fritz had no desire to follow in his father's footsteps. Instead, his passion was to become, of all things, a pastry chef. At that time in Switzerland, such service industry roles were seen as lower-class. As a Sonderegger, Fritz's father insisted he could either be a lawyer or an accountant. But Dr. Robi said his father's can-do, entrepreneurial bent drove him from the start. Even though he came from an extraordinarily wealthy family, Dr. Robi said his father was always innovating and making a buck on the side, for example, collecting people's old skis, thrown away from the season before, and stripping them, painting them, and selling them for the next season. Dr. Robi said,

> He was always doing things like that. Not that he needed the money. It was just in his bones. To this day, he can sell ice to Eskimos. He's just a great character.

Fritz honored his father's wishes to a point by earning a degree in accounting, but he remained determined to strike out on his own. So, in his early twenties, he set off from Switzerland to travel as far away as possible. He ended up in Melbourne, Australia, under the guise of wanting to learn English. Dr. Robi said it was really to escape. Dr. Robi's father was ready and willing to fly the coop and didn't want to be dishonorable by pursuing his passion under his father's roof.

Before Fritz left, his mother gave him a Bible to take on his journey—but not necessarily because she was a devout Christian wanting to pass on a legacy of faith. During that time in Switzerland, Dr. Robi says a person was considered either Protestant or Catholic by default. Still, the gesture was significant enough to Fritz that he read the Bible on the boat to Australia. He concealed it inside the cover of a magazine because he was embarrassed to be seen reading it.

But Fritz's ploy didn't work. Dr. Robi said another passenger noticed.

"Do you know what you're reading?" he asked.

Dr. Robi's father looked up and confessed, "Yes."

"And why are you reading that?"

"To go to heaven," Fritz replied.

The passenger then posed an unexpected question. "Do you know if you are going to heaven?"

Dr. Robi smiled. "That really challenged him," he said of his father, "so when he arrived in Australia, the passenger invited him to church. That's where he met Mom and became a Christian." Mom was Karen, a native of Australia whose family lineage traced back to the Netherlands. He described her as being sweet and the cornerstone, the rock, of their family, a stay-at-home mom who was always there for him and his sister and solid in her faith.

After meeting at church, Fritz and Karen eventually married and were so committed to their Christian faith that they went to Bricket Wood, England, to attend Ambassador College and more deeply study the Bible. They had their first child, Heidi, there in late 1970, and Dr. Robi came along almost two-and-a-half years later. Once they completed their studies, Fritz and Karen decided to travel. Using funds from an inheritance Fritz received when his mother passed away, they headed west, across the pond and to the United States. There, they purchased a Volkswagen camper van and hit the road for the next two years. Dr. Robi said they went everywhere from Florida to Alaska, living as hippies on four dollars a day. But Dr. Robi doesn't remember it. The trek began when he was just two years old.

Soon, though, Heidi needed to start her schooling, and Fritz and Karen returned to Australia and settled in Canberra, the nation's capital. Fritz started an apprenticeship as a pastry chef before founding his own business there called Urambi Hills Bakery. Of the business, Dr. Robi said it was ahead of its time: a whole-meal bakery using organically grown, stone ground, whole meal flour back when everything was white and processed.

Another reason Canberra appealed to Fritz was its proximity to the Snowy Mountains, which was convenient for snow skiing during the winter months.

> A fascinating thing about my father was that he instilled upon us that life is for living—not to be too serious, but to enjoy. If he saw a fresh dusting of snow on the Brindabella Ranges, he'd drive home after the night shift at six a.m., wake up me and my sister, and say, "Come on! We're going skiing because skiing is much more important than school."

Dr. Robi was nine by then, and those fondly remembered excursions with his father into the mountains gave him a love for winter sports. Dr. Robi said,

> I started snowboarding at the age of 11. It was brand new then. I was one of the very first Australians to be snowboarding. But I was also involved in ski racing and belonged to the Australian capital territory ski race squad.

Fritz's "life is for living" mantra wasn't all fun and games, though. Dr. Robi said his father rose at two in the morning to get to the bakery and prepare the breads and pastries in time for morning customers. Most days, he didn't get home until the early afternoon and was already in bed by the time Dr. Robi returned from school. He didn't see his son as often as he'd like, so Fritz invited Dr. Robi to go to work with him a couple of mornings a week.

> He woke me up at two, I went and worked with him, and at eight o'clock in the morning, I went to school. That's just the way it was. We did that for the exclusive reason of spending time together, but it also taught me a work ethic. By the time I was 17, I'd wake up and drive myself in and do the night shift, so that he could take a day off and stay in bed. My father … he always stood on his own feet, running his own business and not working for anyone. That was my role model.

As Dr. Robi entered adulthood, he attended college at Bond University on the Australian Gold Coast, but every December through April he took time off from his studies to travel to Switzerland to earn money as a skiing and snowboarding instructor. During one of those terms away in Switzerland, tragedy struck back home. One night, a gas bottle inside Urambi Hills Bakery exploded, destroying everything. Fritz was injured in the blast with third degree burns on his arms and legs. He recovered and spent approximately $250,000 to rebuild the bakery. But after it reopened, Fritz received a letter from the insurance company. It stated the bottle that exploded was a week past its expiration date. He wasn't covered. This sent him into a financial and mental crisis. Dr. Robi said,

It was financial failure, and in the Swiss cultural context, if you fail financially, you fail period. So, he escaped—as in he literally took off one night and fled. He grabbed his passport and didn't tell anyone where he was going until he got to the airport and called my mom. He said he just couldn't handle it anymore. He took off, and he came to me in Switzerland.

His father's decision was an intriguing twist, considering that Fritz was repeating his own father's cycle. Years earlier, when Dr. Robi was still a small boy, his grandfather Hans fled Switzerland after several unwise investments were wiped out by the United States stock market crash of 1987. By then, Hans and his wife had divorced, and he remarried a German model. Hans was also without most of his vast fortune and couldn't face the shame at home. So he came to Australia to be with Fritz—the very son who'd left home to chase his pastry chef dream. Hans never returned to Switzerland. He lived out his years in Australia.

Fritz spent the next two months in Switzerland with Dr. Robi before they both returned to Australia for his sister Heidi's wedding. Sufficiently recovered from the trauma, Fritz and Karen eventually sold the bakery and their home and moved to Queensland, Australia, to make a fresh start. Meanwhile, Dr. Robi continued his Australia-for-school, Switzerland-for-work routine, earning income at a ski resort in Klosters, Switzerland, as a skiing and snowboarding instructor. Klosters was the go-to destination for a variety of international celebrities, including the British Royal Family. Because he spoke English well and was already head of the snowboarding school there, Dr. Robi was given the opportunity to teach Prince Charles, Prince Harry, and other members of the royal entourage how to snowboard for the first time. That's when Dr. Robi's entrepreneurial leanings, learned from his father, gave him an idea.

Leveraging Opportunity

"I thought maybe there's a way to leverage this opportunity, so I approached a variety of different snowboard and skiwear companies. I was sponsored for my classes, right down to my boots, and the snowboards the princes used were sponsored as well," Dr. Robi said, adding that when the royals fell down, the branding was underneath the board and visible to the photographers.

The royal's snowboard lessons in January 1996 made worldwide headlines, but Dr. Robi's creative sponsorship scheme got him in trouble. Because he benefited financially, it was deemed Dr. Robi took undue advantage of the situation. The princes' secretary from St. James' Palace, and the ski instructor to the royals who was also his boss at the time, told him that when the Royal Family returned the next year, they'd be instructed by someone else. Undeterred, Dr. Robi remained committed to complete college and continued working as an instructor to help pay his way through school.

Fishing for Dinner

Dr. Robi said,

> Because my family had lost their fortune, I literally paid for each semester of college up front. I worked in Switzerland, saved up everything, came back to Australia, and paid my way. I walked out at the end of university without any debt. I was so poor during that period of time, life was challenging. However, I think it helped forge me to become the person that I am today.

He used the small weekly allowance the Australian government provides for students to cover his rent, purchase gasoline, and get food each week: one box of oats to make porridge and one bag of oranges. He'd also visit the nearby canals to study and fish for his dinner. If he didn't catch any fish, there was no dinner.

> But because I was a useless fisherman, I had a lot of time to study. I did so well at my academics, they ended up giving me half of a scholarship. Without having been so impoverished, I would never have gotten a scholarship because I would never have been fishing for my dinner.

At Bond University, Dr. Robi first studied psychology—a field choice that came from a most unusual catalyst.

> I grew up watching a TV show called *Growing Pains* with heartthrob Kurt Cameron as the young stud actor. The dad in the series, Dr. Seaver, was a psychologist. He worked from home, they lived in a really nice house, and he seemed to always have time to hang out with the kids. He was always getting involved in the dramas of the day-to-day life of his family. I thought that would be a cool job: to be a psychologist and work from home, so that's what I pursued.

In addition to school and work, he had also begun snowboard racing. After winning the Australian intervarsity title, he earned a place on the national squad that competed for the world championships and the Olympics.

Sliding Doors Moments

Once his undergraduate classes were completed, Dr. Robi learned that he had been accepted to study his postgraduate honor's degree in psychology at the University of Tasmania, the next required step before he could pursue the master's degree necessary to practice as a clinical psychologist. He was one of only 20 accepted from hundreds of applicants, and he was also compelled to go because Tasmania was home to the Australian Antarctic Research Division. As an adventurer, he wanted to be the first person to snowboard in Antarctica while studying the scientists stationed there. He would research Seasonal Affective Disorder, winter depression, which happens when there is a lack of daylight. Dr. Robi also made the Australian national team and was going to compete at the world championships.

> I had to make a decision. Do I pursue professional snowboarding, or do I pursue psychology as a professional career? It was a sliding doors moment. I had a limited amount of time to make a decision and go through the right door before it closed.

To ponder his choice, Dr. Robi climbed a mountain in Switzerland and found a vantage point to peer out at the majestic view. He asked himself, "Why do I want to go to the Olympics? To represent my country." But then he thought, "Is it really your country that you're representing, or is it yourself?" He had to be honest. If he crossed the line in first, second, or third, and his hands went in the air, would it be for his country's glory or his glory alone?

> Whereas, why would I want to do post-graduate studies? To become a psychologist—and that's to help other people. One was very self-centered, and the other was other-people-centered. I decided to pursue psychology and retire from professional snowboarding. It was a very hard decision to make.

Another sliding doors decision was ahead for Dr. Robi. As he neared completion of his one year of honor's studies at the

University of Tasmania, Dr. Robi was approached to be a celebrity snowboard instructor during the Winter Olympics in Japan. It was an unexpected carryover from his headline-making training with the Royal Family. But by then he had a girlfriend, Noleen, a fellow psychology student also on the verge of graduation.

Prior to beginning this leg of his educational journey, Dr. Robi had committed not to get involved in any romantic relationships. That commitment didn't last long because on the first day of university, Dr. Robi shared,

> I was sitting in the courtyard eating my Vegemite sandwiches, and I saw this girl walking across the courtyard almost in slow motion. I was absolutely captivated, almost intimidated. That's not like me; I'm this confident snowboard instructor from Switzerland. It took me three months to work up the courage to introduce myself to her because I thought I knew she was "the one" and I didn't want to screw it up. When I finally decided to act, I walked up and apologized. I said, "I've been seeing you around for such a long time now, and I just haven't had the courage to come up and introduce myself."

From that awkward beginning, they began dating, but Noleen soon said she couldn't continue the relationship because Dr. Robi wasn't a Christian. Noleen was committed to her faith. While Dr. Robi's parents were believers, too, he had gradually become disenchanted with church. The church of his youth was driven by rules and legalities, including not being able to play sports on Saturdays because Saturday was the Sabbath. He felt he had made significant sacrifices as a kid to be a part of this church.

When I left home and ended up in Switzerland for the first time, that was about the time when our church was doing its own metamorphosis from the inside out. It was like a modern-day reformation. I walked away and drifted over the next couple of years because there was a lot of infighting within the church. When Noleen said she didn't think we could continue our relationship because I'm not a Christian, my response was, "You have no idea. I have earned my right to be called a Christian!" She said, "That statement alone just proves that you're not one."

With her prompting, Dr. Robi began a journey back toward his faith-based roots. He had wandered far away, he said, exploring New Age or Eastern mysticism and meditation. Noleen's observation compelled him to read the Bible.

Because I was on a journey of really taking it seriously to find out what it all means, Noleen gave me a second chance. She saw that I was genuine in my endeavors. She took me to church a couple of times, but I was quite hesitant because I saw people raising their hands. The only other place I'd seen people raising their hands was when a goal was scored in football.

"I always had a faith," he added. "I always believed in God. I just didn't understand what Christianity was really all about." He said he and Noleen often talked about faith in God, "but I wasn't there yet. I was still carrying the legalistic baggage of my youth, of what I grew up with."

Their relationship deepened—so when Dr. Robi got the celebrity snowboard instructor job offer in Japan, he wanted Noleen to join him. But she had helped start an AIDS orphanage in Zambia, Africa, two years earlier and had already committed to returning to the orphanage after her schooling. She told him she was going to Africa. "Then she followed up with, 'I guess you could come with me.' So, needless to say, we went to Africa. Had to follow this girl!"

They spent the next year serving together at the orphanage—but it wasn't the missions work alone that brought on Dr. Robi's greatest sliding doors moment.

> Before I left for Africa, I stole a copy of *The Message Bible* from my dad's bookshelf; I think God forgave me. It was only the New Testament and Psalms and Proverbs, but it was in language I could understand, so I started reading from cover to cover. I got to Romans chapter eight, and I still remember it; I was sitting in the front seat of a car in Zambia riding out to the field wherever we were, and I shut the book and put it down. I had two very strong emotions. One was complete rage. *Why hasn't anyone told me this stuff before? How can I live my whole life, and no one has told me this?* The other, though, was incredible excitement about what I was reading. In that moment, right then and there, I gave my life to Christ, just on my own. I knew this was what I was going to follow for the rest of my days. This was for me. I wanted in.

On their final day in Africa, Dr. Robi and Noleen became engaged to be married—and he looks back today and sees God's purposes being realized through the entire process. He also said he and Noleen saw that they needed more education, so they returned home to get their masters and doctorates.

> We were young and cocky and came out of university thinking we knew it all. Africa humbled us. We

got to see there is so much more we needed to learn to help people shift mindsets because it's not just physical poverty, but mental and emotional poverty that needs to be addressed. It's one thing to fund-raise and give people food and blankets and shelter. It's a whole other thing to help transform mindsets so that they can stand on their own feet.

Changing Plans

Dr. Robi and Noleen were married in December 1999 just after she finished her post-graduate honors studies. He got his doctorate while she worked on her master's degree. They had their first of five children in 2003. Earlier that same year, they moved to the west coast of the South Island of New Zealand, the rugged, picturesque region where the *Lord of the Rings* movies were filmed. While Noleen worked as a clinical psychologist for children and adolescents, Dr. Robi took a year off and just worked part-time as a staff supervisor at the area's hospital.

> I was recovering from my Ph.D. We were pregnant, Noleen was going to stop working, and I was about to start my career. We were thinking to ourselves, "We can go anywhere and do anything. The world is our oyster. We were a force to be reckoned with, two qualified professionals. But where should we go?"

He applied for two psychologist jobs. One was at an ex-pat hospital in China. The other, in Alaska, seemed to him a dream come true: serving the remote villages on the border of Denali National Park. He loved that it required going into the last frontier, somewhere he's never been before, to do something never done before. "I salivate over doing things that have never been conceived of or tried before," Dr. Robi said. "I was made to journey along the road less traveled." He was confident they were heading to Alaska. Around that same time, he was asked to give a keynote presentation back in Brisbane at a conference for the Southbank Institute of TAFE, a technical school in Queensland. His parents had subsequently moved to the Sunshine Coast in Queensland, which is on the east coast of Australia about 90 minutes north of Brisbane. Because of their proximity to Brisbane, Dr. Robi visited his parents.

"On Sunday morning, my mom invited me to church—and God just hit me." He welled up with tears, convinced the Lord was speaking to him about where he should go next, and it wasn't Alaska or China.

> The Holy Spirit tapped me on the shoulder and said, "This is where I am calling you—and not just to this town, but to this church for the next season of life." So, when I returned to New Zealand, I said to Noleen, "You're not going to believe what I'm about to say next, but I think we should go to the Sunshine Coast, start a clinic, and not work for somebody else but start a business ourselves." For me to say that when she knew my heart was for Alaska was a big deal, so she knew that God must have done a number on me to do an about face like that.

He also discovered that God's direction was a relief to Noleen.

> Brand new baby on the way, motherhood, and going to some unknown place in the middle of nowhere versus coming home where family are close by? That was a real bonus to her.

They packed their things and headed northwest, back across the Tasman Sea and to what would become their permanent home. The clinic, called Family Challenge, was launched in Buderim, Queensland, by the end of 2003. It started out of their house after they converted the garage into a clinic. "It was like a home-based business, so I did the Dr. Seaver thing after all," Dr. Robi said with a grin.

A New Enterprise

While Dr. Robi was growing the clinic, Family Challenge began humanitarian projects in Africa by doing community development and leadership training with remote communities in the Copperbelt Region of Zambia. Their projects included everything from supporting a local church to overseeing child sponsorship efforts. They even started their own village in Zambia named after their organization where locals came for meetings, training, women's programs, and a variety of other projects. But in 2004, the Lord challenged Dr. Robi to restructure his organizations so that the business funded their Family Challenge Charitable Trust—turning the clinic into what today is referred to as a social enterprise. Instead of keeping all the profits, he dedicated proceeds from the service to the charity through the charitable trust.

It was a good thing he obeyed God's direction. "On Boxing Day 2004, the big tsunami hit Southeast Asia, and all our donations dried up because everyone gave to relief efforts there," he said, "but thank God, the clinic now funded the charity." That sound decision even allowed Dr. Robi to expand the organization's humanitarian reach that same year into war-torn Northern Uganda to work with children traumatized by being soldiers and sex slaves. "We trained large and small organizations alike from World Vision to Samaritan's Purse on how to educate the children through trauma rehabilitation."

New Methods – Incredible Results

The year he and Noleen spent in Africa had given him a heart for the continent and the plight of its people and prepared him for what was needed in Uganda.

> It got underneath our skin. Then I was watching Oprah Winfrey one day and a nurse was being interviewed who had her daughter abducted by the LRA, the Lord's Resistance Army, and she had started an organization called the Concerned Parents Association to help rehabilitate those who had escaped or been captured and later let go. She was doing trauma rehabilitation—which is what I did my Ph.D. in—so I thought I could help. I flew over to Uganda to meet with them. They said, "We don't know anything about trauma rehab, so we just play loud music and let the kids dance all night long." I thought to myself that it was maybe some kind of dance therapy, but when I started explaining to them how trauma works in the brain and the body, they'd never heard anything like it before. We started training to equip and empower them to use evidence-based treatment programs.

The switch to the new programs was significant, considering the unethical witchcraft practices up to that point, which were endorsed by the United Nations High Commission for Refugees (UNHCR). Dr. Robi revealed that the Lord's Resistance Army was witchcraft-oriented. Girls who were abducted were first smeared with oil to be made bulletproof for combat. They were then told to stand out in the sun, inside a square drawn in the sand, and were required to hold an egg. After several hours, the witch doctor inspected the egg and if there were any bubbles or cracks, the girl was deemed not pure enough for sex and was killed. If her egg was pure, then she was deemed pure enough to be sold as a sex slave and given to a commander as a wife or to be raped. When the children escaped, he said, community organizations would invite their own witch doctors to have what they called "forgiveness ceremonies," where the community forgave the children for what they had done, and instead of holding the egg, they'd crush the egg.

When he asked why they used such unorthodox methods, they said it was so traditional cultural practices could be used as part of the treatment for the trauma. He couldn't believe it, especially considering such practices could retraumatize children and that the modern-day culture of Uganda was based on Christianity, not witchcraft.

> It's not enough to communicate to these children, who have been forced to commit such horrendous atrocities, that the community forgives them. They are the ones who need to learn how to forgive, because unless they do, they will run the risk of becoming the same perpetrators of violence in the next generation, and the cycle of genocide would continue. They need to forgive the government for not protecting them. They need to forgive the rebels for abducting them. They need to forgive us in the West for not caring. There's so many people to forgive, including themselves for what they were required to do.

The new therapy education techniques by Dr. Robi and his team eliminated the witchcraft-based practices—and its success exposed an even greater need for trauma treatment among the 1.7 million refugees scattered in camps along the Uganda-Sudan border. He said there was only one organization, Doctors Without Borders, who had stationed two midwives in one of the 120 camps. It was the only humanitarian organization working in the war zone at that time, he said, because it was just too dangerous to work there. Seeing the demand yet also recognizing the risk, Dr. Robi went to work to come up with a solution that was both designed to succeed and yet wouldn't keep him or his staff needlessly in harm's way.

"We came up with the idea of creating a program that could be standardized, and then we leveraged it by training local indigenous leaders to facilitate. They would take it to their own communities and start to employ it," he said. Leaders came from the cities and townships to receive the training, and Dr. Robi partnered with different existing organizations to make the training available. For example, through one organization called Favor of God, 12 facilitators were taught how to run the program. The program was then launched in September 2006 in a refugee camp housing 65,000 people. "They started groups of 12 people, so a little bit like the disciples, 12 by 12 by 12, within two years, they had 20,000 people who had graduated the program."

The long-term effectiveness of this effort was measured through assessments provided in a partnership with two universities in the United States and Australia. Dr. Robi discovered that the trauma symptoms of the people who had not been through the program continued to get worse, but those who had been through the program—now called Frontline—made a significant recovery from their trauma. "It wasn't just time that healed them; it was the program that made the difference," he said. "We celebrated 100,000 graduates, just in northern Uganda, in 2015. Since 2008, this program has expanded around the world. We are now everywhere, from Eastern Europe and Asia to South America and the Middle East."

Interestingly, Dr. Robi recognized that the same entrepreneurial tendency to leverage opportunity that got him in trouble when training the Royal Family in snowboarding was now being used for incredible good. "We allow the organizations to facilitate it, so we don't have to fund the entire operation on our own. We partner—that's how we try to be as cost-effective as possible," he said, adding that the project in northern Uganda, which cost Family Challenge $200,000 to facilitate, factors down to a cost of only $2.00 a person. Yet, to his knowledge, it's the largest trauma rehabilitation initiative ever undertaken in a war zone.

> We just train up various humanitarian organizations who do this kind of work anyway but don't have the standardized program material. We develop the resources, and then we train the local people who will facilitate the program on the ground. That's our strength.

The development of that strength would soon contribute to his next—and most surprising—sliding doors moment.

More Sliding Doors Moments

With Frontline's success, Dr. Robi was asked in September 2008 to speak at a conference in Uganda. Speaking requests were not unusual for him by then; government and corporate entities coveted his insights on psychology and humanitarian work. As a result, several of his ongoing contracts provided consistent revenue. But this opportunity came from a church-based group in Kampala, Uganda, called Watoto, famous for its world-renowned children's choir and orphanage. Dr. Robi had been there earlier in the year to educate its staff in trauma rehabilitation, and when he was asked to return, it was for the organization's national conference. Wanting to learn more about the event, he found a list of the other invited speakers online. It was a veritable who's who of Christianity. "I had never met these people before," Dr. Robi said, smiling. "I thought to myself, 'Who am I, this random kid from Queensland, who is also speaking at this conference?'"

He spoke on trauma rehabilitation, and thousands of people attended. But it was what Brian Houston, Pastor of Hillsong Church, Australia's largest church, said about the familiar Bible teaching of Jesus building His church that "flew off stage and hit me full force in the chest," Dr. Robi said. "He said, 'Jesus did not say, "I will build my humanitarian organization or my company," not that there's anything wrong with those things, but Jesus said, "I will build my church."

> I really felt God say to me, "I am going to take you out of the world and put you in the church to equip and empower the church," and that was the moment I said, "Noooo! I love the path I'm on." But He obviously had the last word, and that mandate is still with us today.

At the close of the event, Pastor Houston approached him.

> "I know you are really busy," he told me, "but is there any chance that we could get you to Sydney to do some staff training?" I thought, "Staff training is like corporate training." I was trying to justify it in my mind.

The reason Dr. Robi struggled with the opportunity was that he didn't want to get involved in speaking at churches. He knew it would cause a significant reduction of financial gain and believed it could also tarnish his reputation as a professional psychologist in Australia's largely secularized culture.

Nevertheless, with God's directive echoing in his mind, Dr. Robi accepted Pastor Houston's invitation before leaving the conference—only to arrive home to learn that all his government contracts, every last one of them, had been pulled. He was told there had been a policy change, nothing more, but it was clear everything Family Challenge had and would achieve was at a crossroads. "God was sliding shut those doors so that others could open," he said.

He did the training with Pastor Houston's staff, a two-day event from which he was then asked to speak at Hillsong's women's conferences, COLOR. The first was held in Sydney and was followed by events in London, England, and Kiev, Ukraine. Tens of thousands attended, and Dr. Robi was so well received, he was then invited to speak at church events around the world. "This was not my agenda. This was not my plan. God slammed all the doors shut and now all of a sudden I was on some of the biggest platforms in Christendom," he said.

Dr. Robi never charges a fee for his appearances, but churches give him an honorarium and offerings he says are "extraordinarily and extravagantly generous." He, Noleen, and their five children now live exclusively off the income from his speaking opportunities, and his innovative and comprehensive online resources (Dr. Robi App).

He speaks on issues ranging from the psychology of financial independence, apologetics, and mental health to leadership, organizational culture, and family function. His unique ability and distinctive message are rooted in combining the best of science and Scripture. While he believes the popular press has been effective at creating an "artificial narrative" that the Bible and science are incompatible, Dr. Robi challenges anyone to show him peer-reviewed, evidence-based, empirical operational scientific articles that contradict the Bible. He says they simply don't exist.

"In order for something to qualify as empirical operational science, you need to observe it, you need to manipulate it, and you need to replicate it. Most people don't understand this," he said, "or the fact that all science is based and predicated on faith. Everything is based on assumption." He cites the speed of light as an example. It has been empirically measured within our planet's atmosphere. But if asked to determine how long it takes to get from Earth to the nearest exploded star, the answer can only be a guess because the speed of light has never been accurately measured outside of Earth's atmosphere at that distance, and never will be. He said the same lack of empirically measured evidence is true of carbon dating, which he says is based on several assumptions, none of which can be observed, manipulated, or replicated.

Dr. Robi says his best-of-both speaking approach makes sense because he doesn't see himself as a theologian or a pastor, but as a scientist, a clinical psychologist, and a speaker.

> When people invite me to speak, it is because I am a psychologist. They expect a theme which is going to speak into the life of relationships or the life of health, whether it be mentally, emotionally, or behaviorally. But when I look at Scripture lining up so perfectly with evidence-based treatments, it's logical for me to talk from a scientific perspective and validating what Scripture has been saying for thousands of years.

In addition to speaking, Dr. Robi is broadcast regularly on radio and is widely published in both the scientific arena and the popular press.

Global Mental Health Alliance

While he and Noleen continue to operate the Family Challenge clinic with a team of Christian doctors, the Family Challenge Charitable Trust maintains the trauma rehabilitation training work that began in Africa. Dr. Robi is convinced, however, that the Christian church, along with other faith-based humanitarian organizations, can play a more active role in advancing spiritual, emotional, behavioral, relational, and financial health. "The church has both a tremendous opportunity and great responsibility to advance health in its various domains," Dr. Robi said.

Therefore, he says it is necessary for programs to be developed, services offered, and education and training delivered through the church that is not only theologically sound but also scientifically valid (evidence-based, research-driven, and outcome oriented). To ensure and ascertain the effectiveness of these initiatives and interventions, Dr. Robi established the Global Mental Health Alliance to equip and empower Christian churches, faith-based groups, and mental health professionals around the world.

> The Christian church was once the leading global advocate for the advancement of science, the most influential provider of elementary, secondary, and higher education, and the largest provider of healthcare and humanitarian relief. In modern times, however, the church is being stripped of her influence in these domains. Despite being the most notable advocate for healthy marriages and strong families, championing human rights, and preserving the sanctity of life from conception to cessation, the church has been branded as bigoted, narrow-minded, prejudiced, intolerant, and out of touch.

The challenge then, he says, is to reestablish the reputation of the Christian church, enhance the effectiveness of service delivery, and rebuild credibility while avoiding discrimination, marginalization, and legal persecution. He believes the Global Mental Health Alliance achieves this by making churches, faith-based humanitarian organizations, and mental health professionals allies instead of competitors. This helps to strengthen influence, create momentum, and negate obstacles, as recently seen with the launch of a new program called GROW in Northern Iraq.

GROW is a structured educational initiative for the promotion of post-traumatic growth for refugees and survivors of war trauma. A team of mental health experts who all share a biblical worldview has carefully developed the culturally sensitive GROW program over a two-year period.

Since the start of the breakthrough trauma rehabilitation work in Africa, a program Dr. Robi launched entitled EMPOW-ER has been implemented along the border of Northern Uganda and Southern Sudan to continue to help former child sex slaves, child soldiers, and communities impacted by the civil wars there. As originally established, non-professional partners are still empowered to facilitate the program, with seven faith-based organizations facilitating what Dr. Robi calls "emotional resilience training" for the hundreds of thousands of refugees in the region.

Interestingly, it was during the period that both GROW and EMPOWER were developed, from 2010 to 2013, that Dr. Robi and his family traveled extensively—three months in Asia, three months in America, three months back in Australia, and three months in Europe, the same cycle repeated for three years—in support of his speaking opportunities across the world. They employed a nanny and homeschooled their children as they traveled together, but eventually reached a point where Dr. Robi knew they needed to settle down to give the children a more stable home environment. At first, he thought an ideal home would be in the United States at Lake Tahoe straddling the California-Nevada border. They'd even enrolled the children in a private school, but he and Noleen discerned they needed to be certain they were doing what God wanted.

We went to prayer, and Noleen felt that God gave her a Scripture, Jeremiah 16:1. In *The Message* translation, it literally said, "Don't raise a family here." It was as specific as that. We then asked God, "If not here, then where?" And we really felt God say, "Keep reading." Then Jeremiah 16:14-15 said, "As sure as God lives, the God who brought Israel back from the land of the north, brought them back from all the places where he'd scattered them. That's right, I'm going to bring them back to the land I first gave to their ancestors." We just looked at each other and said, "We go to Switzerland!" It was amazing to us.

The move was completed in 2013, and they would stay in Switzerland—until God gave them another divine directive in response to an innovation born from a new global strategy initiative.

Innovations in People Care: A Global Strategy

White Label Project

This strategy involves taking mental health from the frontline and bringing it to the home front. Now through 2020, Dr. Robi says the Global Mental Health Alliance is focusing on "developing and developed worlds alike" to enable churches globally to help strengthen relationships, advance mental health, and promote economic vibrancy. This project, called Innovations in People Care: A Global Strategy, has adopted a "White Label" (neutral in branding) approach to authorship and publishing, making professional resources available for churches without impeding individual/corporate branding and credit.

While expert collaborators on programs are, of course, officially acknowledged for accountability and transparency purposes, as well as to lend authority to respective programs, this project is undertaken in a manner that serves the church without personal agenda. The overarching goal of this initiative is to empower churches around the world to take the lead—to be the head and not the tail—in effectively addressing the world's growing mental, emotional, and relational health pandemic, and to do so in a manner that's economically expedient.

Funding for 34 new Innovations in People Care initiatives has been limited to four investing churches charged with providing support of a $1.5 million budget. Dr. Robi selected churches he felt were innovative and not self-centric or focused on an iconic name or reputation. These churches will have free, lifetime access to all the services and materials offered through Innovations in People Care. Because Dr. Robi wants to make the program affordable for any church that wants to use Innovations in People Care resources, the four investing churches may not get financially reimbursed or otherwise compensated.

To deliver the program's content, modern technology in the form of an app will be used and is now under development. The app's various programs will be coordinated through a designated facilitator at each church. When someone approaches that facilitator for help with a mental health concern, the app will provide resources in three broad areas: health, relationships, and finance. If somebody comes to the facilitator with a relationship concern, for example, the facilitator can press the relationship icon, and it'll generate a drop-down list of subcategory relationship issues. It might be a loss of intimacy, increased conflict, or infidelity. Once initial issues are identified and selected, the facilitator can then press "enter" and receive a tailored and structured quantitative questionnaire. After going through the entire questionnaire with the person, the facilitator can again press "enter" to score and graph the person's current functioning level. Dr. Robi explains there are four categories of functionality: 1) highly functioning, which is where we people should be; 2) average functioning, which is where most people are; 3) challenged functioning, which he says "is the case that the cracks are starting to form in the pavement and the wheels are starting to wobble"; and 4) clinical functioning, where Dr. Robi says "the wheels have fallen off the wagon." That final level, clinical functioning, would be classified as a pathology and outside of the competency of the church unless the facilitator is a trained mental health professional. Once the person's functioning level is determined, Dr. Robi says the facilitator can then use the app to get the individual the educational help they need or refer the person to a professional through an extensive referral network.

A 2.0 version of that app is also being planned that Dr. Robi says will be "self-governed" for young people. In this application, a youth can create his or her own avatar that is male or female, old or young, and from any country and in any language, to serve as their coach or mentor. It'll say, "Hi. How are you doing today?" Then, using artificial intelligence, the avatar will be pre-programmed to respond. "If my answer is, 'I'm not doing so good,' the avatar will respond, 'I am sorry to hear about that. Would you like to talk about it?' If I say 'yes,' the avatar will ask if the problem is in relationships, health, or finance and will ask more questions depending on my response. It'll lead me through to eventually get to the place where it graphs how I am currently functioning," Dr. Robi said.

The inspiration for the app and other services and materials offered through Innovations in People Care came when Rick Perry, the former governor of Texas, inquired of Dr. Robi what role the church could play to advance stronger families, healthier marriages, and greater emotional resiliency through mental health.

> That was the first time anyone actually asked that question, and it affirmed my belief that the church should be the answer. But I knew it must be done in

the right way because I believe the church is not called to counsel people, but to disciple people.

Dr. Robi asked himself,

> So how can we come alongside the church to make sure—when it comes to anxiety, depression, addictions, relationships, parenting, and so on—that help is evidence-based, research-driven, and outcome oriented?

That's when he envisioned developing the standardized structure and electronic spine, in the form of an app, that could be put into the hands of the church globally.

God then orchestrated one more move for Dr. Robi and his family.

> God literally spoke to me in a dream. There was an audible voice, and it said, "If you don't do this project now, I'm going to give it to somebody else." I woke up, and I was alarmed by what the voice had said, knowing that I had been called and commissioned to do this very thing. But secretly, in the back of my mind, I knew that to do it I would need my team of doctors—and that would require me to go back to Australia. I didn't want to do that because my family and I loved being in Switzerland.

True to previous form, though, Dr. Robi overcame his reluctance and made the move. This decision led to yet another innovation—at the very clinic where everything had started his business over a decade earlier.

Psychology Café and Psychology Milk Bar

When Dr. Robi returned to Australia, he discovered that one of the world's leading app developers, who was referred to him for the Innovations for People Care project, was also relocating from London to the Sunshine Coast. Dr. Robi believes God clearly orchestrated the move. To recruit this acclaimed developer and his team, Dr. Robi recognized the need to generate additional capital. He thought about what could be done at the Family Challenge clinic to pioneer newer ways to make its mental health services more attractive and accessible.

As he traveled around the world to meet with various church leaders or people supporting his programs, they'd often say, "Hey, can we get a cup of coffee?" That was a signal to Dr. Robi that they had some issues they wanted to discuss—and it gave him an idea. Using $120,000 of their personal funds and no debt, Dr. Robi and Noleen revamped the clinic to turn it into a café—complete with appropriate décor and lighting, expresso machines, and private booths where patients could meet with psychologists and receive therapy in a coffee-shop type setting. They rebranded the clinic and called it the Psychology Café. Dr. Robi recruited his brother-in-law Matthew to run business operations. Matthew had been married to Dr. Robi's sister Heidi until she passed away from tongue cancer. Additionally, the Grid Trust, through which monies from the Innovations in People Care app will be funneled, was also established as the parent company for the Psychology Café. The café was a success and quickly led to the creation of the Psychology Milk Bar, a 1950s-style diner where kids can meet with their counselors in a fun atmosphere while making and enjoying all-natural milkshakes.

Dr. Robi is investigating ways both the café and milk bar concepts can be tested and replicated nationally or even globally through churches and Christian schools.

Personal Insights

There's no denying that Dr. Robi's entrepreneurial, professional, and spiritual journeys have been intertwined since that day in Africa when he decided he "wanted in" to everything God had to offer through a personal relationship with Him. He identifies Romans and Galatians as the "mental health books" of the Bible, saying they address the hurt, pain, bitterness, resentment, guilt, and shame that many who struggle with mental illness experience.

> Both books talk about the battle between flesh and spirit that happens when we think about developing new habitual patterns of behavior. They're guidebooks for how to overcome—whether it be addictions, compulsions, obsessions, or other challenges. If you pursue things of the spirit, you have less appetite for the flesh. But if you pursue things of the flesh and scratch that rash, then you have less access to the things of the Spirit. It's a dance, a beautiful dance of finding the pathway to liberty and freedom through Jesus Christ.

He also cites Philippians 4:4-8 as the Bible's mental health "mantra." It reads:

> Rejoice in the Lord always. I will say it again: Rejoice! Let your gentleness be evident to all. The Lord is near. Do not be anxious about anything, but in every situation, by prayer and petition, with thanksgiving, present your requests to God. And the peace of God, which transcends all understanding, will guard your hearts and your minds in Christ Jesus. Finally, brothers and sisters, whatever is true, whatever is noble, whatever is right, whatever is pure,

whatever is lovely, whatever is admirable—if any-thing is excellent or praiseworthy—think about such things.

Dr. Robi believes the key to applying this passage lies in a proper understanding of what it means to rejoice.

It's not an emotional state of being. It's an activity. When you rejoice, you are doing something irre-spective of whether you feel like it. And what is that activity? To be anxious for nothing and instead pre-sent your requests and make them known to God with thanksgiving. That thanksgiving, being grate-ful, is the outworking of rejoicing. So even though I can be in the darkest of times, I will praise Him. Then, when you meditate on the things that are right and pure and good, there is this peace that surpasses all understanding. You have a peace where your mind and heart are guarded well.

In addition to heeding the insights from Scripture, Dr. Robi maintains his own mental health with the aid of his wife.

My psychologist is Noleen. She's great. I've learned over the years I need to listen to what this woman says. God speaks to her so clearly that I would be a fool not to take her wise counsel on board.

Their secret weapon as a couple, he says, is prayer.

Our experience has been consistent with what sur-veys have shown. When Christian couples commit to praying, not necessarily for each other but *with* one another, their likelihood of divorce decreases to well under one percent.

Dr. Robi defines praying with each other as an act of communion or "common union" where couples come together in unity to present their common needs to God. "You are a force to be reckoned with because you have a spiritual atmosphere that you are cultivating in your home and your relationship," he said.

As Dr. Robi reflects on all God has enabled him to achieve, while looking ahead at everything that still needs to be done to equip the Christian church to help others be mentally well, he is increasingly driven to accomplish God's will and fulfill His purpose on Earth.

> I want my life to count. I want it to be meaningful. I want to leave a legacy where people could say mine was a life worth lived because it benefited others. I guess that's what we all want, to ultimately stand before our Lord and hear those words, "Well done, good and faithful servant."

When asked to pinpoint his *why*, Dr. Robi responded, "Why not?" It is not a flippant, "Why not," but rather a contemplative and sincere statement of purpose.

Dr. Robi recalled what he learned years ago while listening to Dr. Myles Munroe during his first trip to Africa with Noleen.

> Dr. Miles' first message was all about purpose. He said that circumstances are always changing, but God's principles are universal; they are timeless. For me, the principle of purpose is to use the gifts, talent, and resources that God has given me while applying the knowledge to which He has graciously led me, so I can contribute to His kingdom in a manner that is bigger than myself and is pleasing to Him. The only way that I can do that is to trust God completely and follow wherever He leads me be-

cause, as I have learned, His plan for me is much bigger and better than I could ever conceive or achieve on my own.

Dr. Robi continued,

It won't eliminate our human challenges and difficulties, but if we choose to follow, God will guide us down the wonderful path He has prepared for us. In addition to taking us to marvelous and exciting places we have never been before and would never go on our own, He enables us to accomplish things well beyond our singular abilities. God's path leads to inner peace and fulfillment, and ultimately to eternal life with the author and creator of the universe who loves us so deeply that He gave His only son so that through His grace we can be one with Him—forever! After considering the alternatives, it is easy for me to say, "Why not! I'm all in!"

Personal Reflection and Group Discussion

1. Dr. Robi had to make a very difficult choice between pursuing professional snowboarding or psychology. He referred to it as a "sliding doors" moment because he had limited time to make a decision and go through the right door before it closed. His decision came down to assessing his motives. What "sliding doors" moments have you faced? In hindsight, did you choose to pursue God's will? If yes, how has your choice changed the trajectory of your life? If not, how will you approach these "sliding doors" moments in the future to assure that your choice is aligned with God's will?

2. The simple act of reading the Bible played pivotal roles in the lives of both Dr. Robi and his father. In what ways has your reading of Scripture impacted you? Your family? Your business?

3. In clinical psychology, those in need are typically served one person at a time, or, at best, in small groups. Yet Dr. Robi has been led by God to innovatively leverage his talent and gifts to help transform the mindsets and improve the lives of hundreds of those in need. Have you persistently sought God's direction in how you might leverage your or your company's capabilities and talents to serve and improve the lives of others?

4. Dr. Robi states that the secret weapon in his vibrant and happy marriage to Noleen is prayer. In addition to their individual prayer time, they pray with each other daily, coming together to present their common needs to God. Dr. Robi conveys, "You are a force to be reckoned with because you have a spiritual atmosphere that you are cultivating in your home and your relationship." If you are married, do you invest time praying together with your spouse? If not, will you give it a try?

5. About rejoicing, Dr. Robi said, "It's not an emotional state of being. It's an activity." How have you made rejoicing in God an activity in your personal life? In your professional life?

6. What other spiritual, business, and personal concepts and practices noted in this chapter stood out to you? How will you integrate them into your life and/or business?

3

Bumpuku: Jacto Agricola

Pompéia, Brazil

"It is always necessary," Shunji Nishimura said, "to sow more seeds for life." This is the story of Shunji's legacy as seen through his life and that of his son, Jorge. It is the story of the fruit that one seed can bear.

Shunji's last project in his community before he died in 2010 at the age of 99 was to help older Japanese inhabitants, who otherwise would have nothing else to do, start gardens and make ceramics. Yet the seed of Shunji's legacy started to take root during the Showa financial crisis in Japan in 1927.

Following World War I, Japanese companies invested heavily to increase production in support of a post-war business boom. However, a post-1920 economic slowdown followed by the Great Kanto earthquake in 1923 led to an economic depression and the failure of many businesses. To stabilize the country's overextended banks, the government intervened through the bank of Japan by issuing discounted "earthquake bonds." In 1927, the government proposed that these bonds be redeemed. Rumors spread that the banks holding these bonds were going to go bankrupt, and a run on the banks began. Thirty-seven banks, mostly smaller ones, went under.

As a result of this crisis, the economy ground to a halt. Many businesses closed, and there weren't enough jobs to support most Japanese families. Shunji and his family were farmers in the Uji region, Japan's oldest farming area known for its fine-quality tea leaves. The Nishimura family's livelihood was devastated by the depression. Japanese tradition called for the oldest son to stay home and take care of the parents, for which he received the inheritance. The second son was invited to leave the home and find work to support himself and help to support the family financially. Shunji was the second Nishimura son.

The Nihon Rikkokai Mission was a Japanese Christian organization founded by U.S. missionaries in 1903 to aid the Japanese people in finding work and then immigrating to the United States and other countries. Shunji connected with them in 1931, but the United States was in the grips of its own economic depression and had few jobs for its own citizens, much less for immigrants. The opportunity Rikkokai offered Shunji, therefore, was in Brazil.

A country with a rich history and agricultural economy that is now one of the world's leading exporters of agricultural products, Brazil has also faced more than its share of crises. First colonized by the Portuguese in 1500, Brazil abolished slavery in 1888 and experienced a shortage of laborers to work the fields. This led to the recruitment of Europeans and, later, of Japanese to provide field labor.

On February 6, 1932, at the age of 21, Shunji boarded the ship Buenos Aires Maru in the port of Kobe, Japan and departed for Brazil. He had a technical degree, carried a Bible, and had 100 yen in his pocket, which was borrowed money given to him by his father (the approximate equivalent of $556 USD in 2015). Shunji arrived in Santos, Brazil on March 22 and immediately went to work as a farmhand harvesting coffee in Botucatu, a small agricultural city in the state of São Paulo. He earned enough to repay his transportation costs, and he saved enough to go to school in São Paulo to learn Portuguese.

Shunji took on a variety of odd jobs to cover his meager expenses, including being a waiter and repairing small machinery. He adopted Brazil as his home, and in 1935 at church, he met his future wife, Chieko, who was also Japanese. They wed the following year and had a daughter, Matiko, in 1937. They settled in the rural agricultural town of Pompéia the next year. Located nearly 300 miles west of São Paulo, Pompéia was the last railroad stop in the state and had a population under 20,000. Shunji opened a modest "fix all" shop where he repaired tools and household equipment. He and Chieko had six additional children from 1939 to 1953, with Jorge being the youngest.

From day one, Shunji insisted on a way of life ruled by his strong Christian and Japanese values. They were simple and straightforward: Believe in God, Keep Your Family Together, Make Friends, Work Hard, and Always Be Honest. Of utmost importance, too, was protecting his family's honor by doing what he said he was going to do. He guaranteed the quality of his work and then stood behind that guarantee.

One day, Shunji was presented with a new challenge—an agricultural "duster" in need of repair. This rudimentary farm implement was hand carried by the laborer and used to dispense powdered crop chemicals. Shunji repaired the duster and decided to learn more about his customer's farm equipment. In the process, Shunji started designing and building products to better meet the needs of his rural farmer customers. His first invention was an improved duster, one that could be worn on the farmhands' backs. It was built by hand, used a kerosene fuel container to hold the powder, and had a tube for dusting the chemicals. He gave it canvas straps so it could be carried like a backpack and a long hand crank that, when operated, sprayed the powder where directed.

While conveying his father's story, Jorge said, "In a land of blind people, the man with one eye is king," adding that his father "was the ultimate entrepreneur who always had an eye for technology and innovation." Shunji's new invention led to the founding of Jacto Agrícola in 1948. Jacto means "jet" in Portuguese, and Shunji derived this name from the trails of white powder the sprayer left behind that looked like the contrails produced by jet exhaust at high altitudes.

Like jet aircraft companies back then, Jacto was a highly innovative company under Shunji's leadership. His eye for the future was evident even in the early days of Jacto. When liquid agricultural chemicals began replacing their powdered counterparts, Jacto created new liquid sprayers. When Shunji became aware of the use of plastic for commercial use, he traveled to Germany to learn more about it so he could make his sprayer tanks lighter by converting them from metal to plastic. Shunji eventually started his own plastics company, Unipac, which has become a well-known and respected supplier of plastic products and parts to many industries. Through an ongoing series of mechanical and technological innovations and inventions, Jacto grew to what is today Máquinas Agrícolas Jacto S.A. (Agricultural Machinery Jacto S.A.), a company that now spans six continents.

In 1971 at age 61, Shunji passed the day-to-day management of Jacto to his son Jiro, and eight years later, stepped down as chairman of the company at the pinnacle of his career. In just over 30 years, Jacto had become an exporter of its products, founded the plastics company Unipac, and launched a transportation and logistics company called Rodojacto. During this period, Jacto debuted the first mechanical coffee harvester in the world and established the Fundacão Shunji Nishimura (Shunji Nishimura Foundation).

Sowing More Seeds for Life

Shunji now had a new goal to pursue: his passion and vision to educate 500 agricultural technicians about everything necessary to run a farm—from using the right equipment to applying the appropriate technology and managing the business. He devoted his time exclusively to this new educational project funded and operated through the nonprofit technology branch of his foundation. Shunji's motive was merely to give back to Brazil. The country had allowed him to immigrate, and its people had accepted him and supported his growth. He had a grateful heart and wanted to do more to elevate his country.

Over the remaining 30 years of Shunji's life, the foundation's schools surpassed his original goal, training more than 700 agricultural students. Several thousand more have been educated since his death. The foundation also supports the Shunji Nishimura School, which serves grades kindergarten through ninth on its separate campus in Pompéia. The mission of the school is to contribute to the overall development of its students with an education based on moral values and ethical attitudes.

It is nothing short of impressive to tour the technologically-advanced campus of the Shunji Nishimura Technology Foundation. His dream has grown into a modern campus that covers over 200 acres and includes the facilities and staff for four different schools and programs. Each school and program serves Brazil with a distinct and unique purpose.

Senai Shunji Nishimura School is the equivalent of a vocational school that advances those already working in the agricultural labor market by offering proficiency improvement courses and specialization training. It also offers an apprenticeship course for those seeking training for their first job. In 2015, the school had over 2,000 students enrolled in its various courses. Additionally, the foundation has formed a bridge program with Senai and the Master's Academy in Canada to create an innovative high school program in Pompéia.

FATEC Shunji Nishimura was founded in 2009 and is a college-level technology school for students who are new to the industry. It offers free courses that focus on the innovative use of technology in farming, including GPS, robotics, and customized software. The three-year program accepts 80 new students every semester and has over 1,200 graduates. The program is a substantial contributor to Brazil's agricultural economy. Graduates from its first eight classes were selected for positions in 170 cities in 11 Brazilian states.

Soil Laboratory was deployed in 1985 and provides services for farmers in the chemical and physical analysis of soil to determine fertility, and in the chemical analysis of plant tissue. The laboratory performs about 40,000 analyses per year throughout Brazil. The lab also helps teachers and students conduct experiments and provides supervised internships.

The Volunteer Program is an offshoot of Shunji's last project to help older Japanese inhabitants of his community. It involves people of all ages and organizes and promotes service to the participants' communities and neighbors.

As a result of a grateful heart, giving back seems to be innate within the Nishimura family DNA, an essential part of Shunji's legacy. With purpose and innovation from kindergarten through college, and in preparing and retraining work forces, their foundation continues to perpetuate Shunji's example of sowing more seeds for life.

Things Don't Always Go as Planned

Shunji and his family built Jacto into one of the 500 largest companies in Brazil by the time of his death in 2010. Shunji was highly recognized and decorated by those within his industry, by the Brazilian government, and by local governments and organizations throughout the country. Yet Shunji never lost sight of his family and the need to unite around a shared vision. Jorge said,

> If you have shared vision for the future, you have peace in the organization. Everyone has a point they can see and work toward together. It is important to dedicate time and resources to this vision, as the vision will always be changing as you progress forward. The mission and values remain constant, but the vision changes.

Achieving unity around a shared vision wasn't always easy. Outside forces seemed to work against the family, and one crisis after another struck. Through the 1980s and early 1990s, the Brazilian economy was under tremendous strain. It suffered from economic stagnation and then rampant inflation that ballooned to more than 225 percent in 1985 and peaked at a staggering record average annual rate of 2,952 percent in 1994. During these years of crisis, it was practically impossible for a business to make money. Shunji was afraid they were going to lose everything.

In 1992, with Jacto on the brink of failure, Shunji called the family together to vote on who should be president, something often referred to today as a vote of confidence. Serving as president at the time was Shunji's son Jiro, to whom Shunji passed the role in 1971. Serving alongside Jiro was Jorge.

After graduating from college in 1976, Jorge went to work in Germany to gain international work experience. He returned to Brazil in 1981 and started a small business within the Jacto Group which he operated for five years. In 1987, Jiro asked Jorge to join him at Jacto, and they worked together as a team from that point forward. Yet on that fateful day in 1992, Jiro and Jorge were fired by their father and brothers. Their brother Takashi became the new president and served in that role until 2001.

Jorge was stunned. Only two months earlier, he had read and been profoundly moved by a book on the Beatitudes (Matthew 5:1-12). With the understanding that everything good comes from God, Jorge had prayed deeply and opened his heart and hands to God—to freely give and receive as God willed. This was a time of great joy and of internal peace when Jorge learned that only God can provide when we give ourselves to Him. Now, he had been terminated from his job and was completely bewildered about what God was doing. His faith was shaken. What Jorge did not see or understand then was that the Lord had prepared him perfectly for this time and situation and was molding Jorge for his future calling.

Jorge met his future wife, Marcia, at a church youth camp in 1973. Marcia's family was also from Japan and had come to Brazil to work in the coffee industry. Jorge, then 20, was immediately smitten, and it didn't take long for him to announce to Marcia that he was looking for a wife, not a date—and that God had given him a vision she was *the one*! It was a bold declaration considering that Marcia was already engaged to someone else at the time. She informed Jorge that God needed to tell her the same thing through her father. Later, when Jorge came to meet Marcia's family for the first time, he brought fresh watermelon for everyone to share. This act of kindness was well received, and they were soon married.

In the mid-1980s, Marcia suffered from depression. Neither Marcia nor Jorge knew much about the condition, but they did some research and were led to participate in a marriage enrichment ministry, Nova Shalom (meaning "new peace"), offered through their church. Together, they began to find a depth of love and peace in their marriage they had not previously experienced, and as their relationship strengthened, her depression lessened. Apparently, God needed Jorge and Marcia to be at peace in their relationship to prepare Jorge to lead his family toward new peace in Him.

By 1987, Jorge and Marcia began leading small groups of married couples in their home using the Nova Shalom program. Their transparency about their relationship struggles, combined with the program content, helped others to deal with their marriage issues. As they sowed seeds of peace, Jorge and Marcia watched the roots of their union grow deeper.

After Jorge was fired in 1992, his faith commanded him to forgive even though he was bewildered and hurt. He prayed for a forgiving heart and found peace. He did not fight back. He decided to lean on his trust in the Lord and follow wherever God led him. Still, there were times that he confessed, "I needed some oxygen."

Later that year, Jorge and Marcia decided to travel to the United States to Nova Shalom's annual international conference. They were warmly received, and unconditional love for them was sincerely expressed. After the founder of Nova Shalom got to know Jorge and Marcia and saw their servant hearts, he asked them to become the national leaders for the marriage ministry in Brazil. The couple was astonished by the invitation. He was a business owner; she was a wife and mother. They didn't know anything about running a ministry.

Although Jorge had returned to running the small company he had founded prior to joining Jiro at Jacto, he did have some time available. They didn't understand why or how it made any sense, but Jorge and Marcia prayed about it together and felt God was calling them to go deeper with the ministry. A self-described "practical guy," Jorge reasoned that, if they failed, the damage was likely to be minimal. They agreed to accept the position, returned home, and with the support of the pastors from their local churches, immediately began working to strengthen marriages throughout Brazil.

The first year was an uphill climb. They had to do everything: prepare the materials, lead their own groups, and identify participants with leadership abilities and train them. This was all done in their home during the evenings and on weekends. Their three children—Stefan Dyo, Theo Shodi, and Melissa Yuko—were also required to pitch in to help. It was hard work, but it was gratifying to experience the marriages being saved as a result. Jorge and Marcia's oldest son, Stefan, said,

> My siblings and I learned from our parents to use our time, talent, and resources to help others. We watched them give almost every weekend to expanding their ministry for others' benefit.

In the first year, the couple and the leaders they recruited and trained successfully facilitated 50 groups of seven couples each. By the end of year two, the number doubled. Within five years, over 1,000 groups were underway, giving Nova Shalom more couples involved in marriage enrichment groups in Brazil than even in the United States.

While the early 1990s birthed a time of growth for Jorge and Marcia, the Brazilian economy continued to falter, and the Nishimura family business was still losing money and headed toward insolvency. The turmoil almost split the family and the company along with them. Yet God had other plans! The two who had been fired, Jiro and Jorge, were the two practicing Christians among the siblings, and they knew they had to forgive and not harbor any resentment or bitterness. They were still involved with Jacto as shareholders, and if the business was to be saved, they knew family harmony had to be restored first. During a family business meeting in 1994, someone suggested they elect a coordinator to help the family repair their divisions and restore their unity. There was a vote, and Jorge was elected to the role.

It was then that Jorge realized that God's hand had been in his firing all along. He believes he was chosen for the new role because he did not fight back but, instead, forgave. His family also observed the confidence and humility he possessed in restoring relationships through his marriage enrichment ministry with Nova Shalom. His family had witnessed Jorge becoming a peacemaker, and even though it is unusual in the Japanese culture for a younger brother to be placed in a position of leadership by the older siblings, that is exactly what happened. Nearly seven years later, Jorge became the board chairman for the family's business holdings. "It's not just about how to solve the problem," Jorge said. "It is also about how to bring people together and unite in doing so."

Jorge had given it all to God and was committed to trusting Him in all matters. Looking back, Jorge understands that he would have never left Jacto on his own accord. If he hadn't been fired, he and Marcia would have never attended the Nova Shalom conference and ended up building a marriage enrichment ministry. In learning and teaching others about the marriage covenant, Jorge had come to understand the importance of covenant for his family and their company.

One of the beatitudes discussed in the book that led to Jorge's heartfelt prayer and commitment to God states, "Blessed are the meek." Jorge is confident that his work in ministry and with the family became welded together as one because he had opened his hands and heart to God's will and had dealt with the business and family crisis with humility. His motives were pure and sincere. God had been preparing Jorge to lead his family with purpose. "The intersection of ministry and business is a powerful combination," added Jorge's son Stefan.

Unity Around Purpose

Uniting family members after a debilitating financial and emotional crisis was a challenge, and Shunji decided outside perspective was needed to help them understand the importance of standing together. He brought in a friend from Japan who knew the family and in whom the family trusted. In his first meeting with the family, Shunji's friend (though not a Christian) quoted 1 Corinthians 13:4-8a from the Bible to remind the family why they should be unified:

> Love is patient, love is kind. It does not envy, it does not boast, it is not proud. It does not dishonor others, it is not self-seeking, it is not easily angered, it keeps no record of wrongs. Love does not delight in evil but rejoices with the truth. It always protects, always trusts, always hopes, always perseveres. Love never fails.

He worked individually and collectively with everyone and ultimately proposed that they make a covenant to stay together and work through their problems. A photo was taken that day of the family standing hand-in-hand to commemorate their covenant. It was an important first step for a family that honors its commitments.

The five brothers involved in the business decided to act on their new covenant by spending a week together to work through their differences. They went away to a hotel to figure out how to move forward in unison. On the first day, only five minutes into the meeting, two of the brothers got into an argument—and everyone went their separate ways. They were disappointed, Jorge said, but they wouldn't give up. "Perseverance is part of our family's DNA," he said.

It was clear they needed help from a third-party facilitator. They hired a consultant and started meeting with him once a month. He convinced them that they wouldn't make any progress until they figured out how to relate to one another and make decisions as shareholders. The siblings formally agreed to accept nothing less than a unanimous vote regarding how the business was to be governed, and it took most of the next year for them to achieve and document the desired consensus. As they went through the process and reached points of agreement, they noticed how their stress and anxiety diminished. As the family's harmony improved, so did their ability to run and turn around the business. When the Shareholder Agreement was finally completed, Jacto was once again moving in the right direction—and so was the Nishimura family. But how could they ensure that this newfound unity wouldn't be lost in a future crisis?

As coordinator of the board, Jorge then began looking to other family-owned businesses for best practices on how to operate, grow, and transition a business through the generations. It was a prudent decision as less than 15 percent of family businesses continue family ownership through the third generation.[1] Jorge, the family peacemaker, developed a PEACE process for Jacto. Since then, it has been the go-to guide for the development and documentation of business best practices and family governance strategies. PEACE is an acronym that abides by the following processes.

P is for *planning*. Each company in Jacto goes through an annual strategic planning process that includes creating a new short-term vision (three years) and long-term vision (10 years).

E is for *emotional and spiritual balance*, primarily evidenced through forgiveness, love, and covenant (strong ties). The need for this component became evident during the business and family crisis they had just overcome.

A is for *agreement*. Working on the Shareholder Agreement expanded into documentation of the family values and to a third-generation project currently underway called Acordo Sociofamiliar (Social Family Agreement) that will clarify how the third generation will work together to govern the family holdings in a manner that promotes the core family values and successfully perpetuates the governance structure.

C is for *character*. The family decided to document their company values in order to affirm who they are in business and what they value. It was not an exercise about who they thought they should be. Rather, it made clear the core of their character and why it was important for their future as a business and as a family. The Nishimuras strive to convey these values primarily through their example. "If you say something," Jorge said, "do it."

E is for *estrutura organizational* (corporate governance). The focus here was to spell out the different levels of leadership and what types of decisions should be made at each level. Jorge explained,

> This is critical because, without clear structure, you will have confusion. The structure was developed and has been continually refined over the years to fit the changes in the vision without compromising their purpose and/or core values.

Jorge continued,

> We gained unity in our organization by bringing the shareholders, board, and top managers together in building and documenting our Purpose, Vision, and Values. We maintain unity by having the same parties involved in our process of refining our short- and long-term vision and in the corresponding adjustments to our corporate-governance structure. This is a living process that will never be finished.

Jacto's non-family leadership team is comprised of talented individuals who are united in their dedication to upholding Jacto's culture. Each one considers the commitment to these values to be a sacred covenant. They insist that the organization represent these values without compromise. Leadership team member and foundation director Alberto Issamu Honda said,

> People from the outside hear about our company and its values and seek employment here over large multi-national companies. We are able to attract people who have good values.

Fellow team member Tsen Chung Kang added,

> As Christians, we get our direction from the Lord. One of our basic principles is that we have to trust and wait on the Lord and make decisions accordingly.

Shin Nagumo, team member and president of Jacto's Business Unit Council, said,

> The values of our company are Christian values that tie everything together—business, education, the

foundation, and personal development. We think in terms of having everything work together. The values are documented and lived by our leaders. They are not just words.

Core Values

The family and non-family leadership team worked together to develop the following ten core values for Jacto.

1: Three Virtueties

Virtueties is a word created by Jorge, which refers to honesty, humility, and simplicity.

2: Happy Customer

Jorge stated that this is the company's "reason to exist."

3: Work Hard in Order to Thrive

Jorge said,

> What you work hard to receive you hold onto. What comes easy goes easy. This is a long-term mindset connected to father.

4: Social and Environmental Responsibility

Social responsibility, Jorge says, is from "God's second-greatest commandment to love our neighbor as ourselves." He said environmental responsibility "is how we show our love for God by lovingly caring for His creation. Both are very relevant to us, not just words on a wishing well."

5: Developing Our People

According to Jorge's son Stefan, the greatest challenge is to find people with similar values. Stefan said, "We are focused on growing our future leaders from within. This focus shows we care about our people." As an example of honoring this value, the family promoted from within to appoint Fernando Gonçalves Neto as company president in 2014. Today, each of Jacto's business entities is led by a non-family member. In addition, Jorge said Jacto avoids taking people from other companies by offering higher pay.

> We believe that, if you entice someone away from another company, you are coveting; it is a sin. If someone approaches Jacto for a job opening, and that person is currently employed, we ask their employer if they will release the employee and give us permission to hire him or her.

6: Nobody Grows Alone

Jorge said Jacto understands that it is part of a larger ecosystem.

> This value applies to everyone within the ecosystem—farmers, dealers, suppliers, partners, and ourselves. We are not self-sufficient. When you humble yourself and ask God and others for help, they will gladly do so. If you are not humble, but rather "the star guy" with a full cup, there is no room for help. When we ask how we can help them grow, people get excited because it shows we care.

7: Innovative Spirit

Making sure farmers have access to technologies that make them more competitive and able to optimize their production is Jacto's commitment. Jorge said,

> It is known as "the Jacto Way" and is a huge competitive advantage. The excitement to discover new ways to do things is within everyone. It is up to the company to provide the environment in which they are encouraged and challenged to do so.

He added that, if Jacto doesn't innovate,

> ...we start to become obsolete because, if we don't do it, someone else will. To create is to take responsibility. Creating begets ownership. We work to create an environment for people to have the freedom to be innovative. But you can't give freedom without clear values.

8: Avoiding Debt

In the 1970s, Jorge said Jacto was in debt to the degree that two-thirds of its profits were needed just to pay interest. In 1981, Shunji decided to get the company out of debt and stay out—and it was debt free within two years.

> In 2007, we decided to keep at least two-month's revenue in cash as capital reserves. Today, the company has enough in strategic cash reserves to service the company's expenses for twelve months with no revenue. Being debt free with significant cash reserves enables us to determine our destiny and continue to improve—no matter what.

As an example, Jorge cited how the company had the money to invest in an extensive and expensive new systems, applications, and products software system, even when Brazil was in an economic crisis.

> Our people also had the time to implement the new system because there was no pressure on production. There have been a couple of times during economic crisis in Brazil that we have earned more on the interest of our capital reserves than the company earned before the crisis!

9: Honoring Commitments

Jorge calls this, "Simply doing what we say we will do." Jacto has made mistakes, he said, but everybody in the marketplace knows the company will do its best to make it right.

> It was one of the starting points for our company. Father's sprayers were handmade and would sometimes break, but he always repaired them. It wasn't just the machine but, more importantly, the guy behind the machine. This value also applies to paying our bills and financial commitments on time.

10: "Happiness in Sharing"

The consensus among the company's leadership team is that the most important goal in looking to the future is to transfer these core values to the next generation of leaders, managers, and workers. Jorge said,

> In our company, we strive to keep the spiritual, moral, and ethical values as true treasures because we depend on them as fundamental keys for the

survival and continuity of the company through the generations. The key to doing so is to understand biblical principles and commandments and to honor and not violate them in all we do. The good decisions to honor God bless you for life. The bad decisions will ultimately harm you even though you may seem to be doing well. I believe this because my family and I are harvesting the fruit from honoring God, His commandments, and His biblical principles.

No Compromise

But success hasn't come easily. Brazil remains a country in continual economic and political crisis. The most recent economic crisis began in 2014 when the government discontinued subsidizing low-interest loans to farmers and other businesses. Interest rates soared, and by 2015, an individual with credit-card debt paid a monthly interest rate that equated to 220 percent per year. Business loans, if you could get one, were at more than 30 percent, and interest paid on deposit at banks was around 11 percent. This was followed by crippling political upheaval fueled by corruption at the highest levels of government and business. To maintain a successful business committed to exemplifying biblical principles in this type of environment has been possible, Jorge says, because of the Nishimura family's commitment to their core values.

> First, we simply won't do business with corrupt entities or people. Our principles are more important than money. We won't compromise our principles. Truth is truth and always rises to the surface.
>
> Second, crisis can be healthy if you have a strong foundation. Like a tree with deep roots, a

company with a strong foundation can survive a drought.

Because our foundation is strong, we grow during crisis. We get sharper and continue to work with farmers and our dealers; invest in research, development, and innovation; and look for ways to improve our efficiency and quality. When the crisis ends, we have a significant advantage because our competitors have had to cut back due to their debt loads while we have invested in progress and innovation. We also earn a lot of interest on our financial reserves because interest rates are so high.

Today, Jacto's annual revenue is approximately $400 million, depending on the exchange rate and economic conditions. They are known for the superior quality of their products and their collaborative approach with their farmer customers and the dealers through whom they sell and service their equipment. Jacto and the Nishimura family have won numerous awards and received tremendous recognition throughout Brazil for their contributions to their industry, the country, and most importantly, to the farmers they serve.

In 2013, Jacto Agricola was presented with the *Globo Rural Magazine* "Best Company" award in the tractors and agricultural machinery segment. That same evening, it was named "Champion of Champions" among the top companies in the 20 agribusiness segments. During his acceptance speech, Jorge had the opportunity to point out that "nobody grows alone," sharing a tribute to Jacto's staff and all its stakeholders.

Touring the Jacto Agricola manufacturing facility instills an appreciation for the complexity with which they work. It is a unique combination of innovative manufacturing processes and systems, the logistics of integrating a multitude of building components, and the incorporation of cutting-edge technology. Most impressive is that the manufacturing facility is pristinely clean and organized to near perfection. Sitting in the driver's seat of one of their newly-manufactured large-crop sprayers feels like being in the cockpit of a modern jet. While it has a steering wheel, it can literally drive itself using GPS and robotic technology. There are computer monitors, switches and dials, instrument panels, and joysticks for mechanism control. The machine can automatically adjust the amount of spray applied based on different soil conditions and can simultaneously adapt to differing terrains and plant height.

The amount of technology and innovation built into the sprayer is astounding, the result of one of Jacto's most important groups, the Innovation Committee. It is charged with the enormous responsibility of ensuring that Jacto continually innovates products, methods, and resources that help the farmer and their partnering dealers progress and make a profit.

Preparing the Next Generation

According to Jorge, the greatest ongoing challenge now for Jacto is to transfer the values and culture to the coming generations and that the family's governance of the organization endow the necessary leadership.

> My generation looked for opportunities. The new generation has lots of options. As our family gets larger, it is very different in personality. But we must remain very similar in values. While becoming vastly different in interests and personality, if we can continue to transfer them from one generation to the next, our family will always have the most important thing in common—our values!

The process began in 1995 when Shunji shared with the 19 third-generation family members the company's history and the importance of planning in continuing the company and its culture. Jorge and his four living brothers (Lincoln passed away in 2009) are all owners in the family holdings. Each family branch decides when and how to pass shares to their heirs. The driving force behind documenting the core values and creating the governance structure in 2004 was to establish the purpose and methodology for continuing family unity, family values, and the family enterprises through the generations. Jorge said,

> We knew our third generation was not yet ready to take over management of the companies. We had an urgency to get them ready by the time the second generation reached age 65, the compulsory age of retirement from operational positions. Accordingly, in 2004, we developed a long-term transition and governance plan and started implementing it immediately.

He said this plan established three main goals: consolidation of corporate governance, professionalization of management, and preparation of the third generation as shareholders. Jorge believes the third generation understands that their successful stewardship will be dependent upon a different set of skills and knowledge than those required to be a successful manager or leader at the operational level.

> The process through which the third generation is being led is also designed to help them see the big picture and connect the dots of how one decision can affect all of the pieces.

While the second generation is guiding the third generation, it is the third generation that is now taking the responsibility to work together and create the agreement. Ten of the third- generation family members are active in the governance process, with five on the Family Governance Council and five serving at the operational level.

The following governance entities were put in place and have become an integral part of the business oversight. Each council has detailed written policies, procedures, and purpose statements.

Family Governance Council (FGC)

It is focused on family and shareholder unity and issues, not the business operations. Each family branch elects two members to the Family Governance Council. "The number-one issue that family businesses must solve is conflict," Jorge said, noting that two-thirds of failures of family businesses are caused by inter-family conflict. The FGC is where questions are raised and discussed and potential areas of conflict are addressed and resolved.

UJI Holding Council

This entity's focus is governance of the family-business holdings. Each family unit assigns one member and one alternate councilor to the UJI Holding Council.

The UJI Holding Council is supported by three additional governance councils that get involved directly in the day-to-day oversight and planning for the various companies and their educational and social endeavors. The *Administrative Council* oversees the governance for the primary business units: Jacto Agricola, Unipac, Sintegra, Multijacto Argentina, and Jacto Small Farms Solutions in Brazil, Thailand, and the United States. The *Business Unit Council* is responsible for the other business units: JactoClean, Rodojacto, Mizumo, Veículos Jacto, Ferramentaria Jacto, and Fundicão Jacto. The *Curator Council* oversees all of the activities of the foundation.

There is no CEO over all of the enterprises. Rather, each business unit has a president or manager focused solely on his or her business unit. There is absolute clarity at every level regarding what decisions are to be made by each.

In addition to guiding the family governance process, Jorge and Marcia transitioned their nationwide marriage enrichment ministry, Nova Shalom. They went from solely providing biblically-based marriage training to focusing on training for the entire family. Jorge did this by connecting what he calls the "Seven Mountains of Influence" (i.e. family, education, religion, business, government, arts and entertainment, and media).

> You can't isolate them. You need to link all seven mountains. When you do so and they all work together, you get transformation. We have a holistic view that there is much more strength if you are part of a connected ecosystem.

Jorge and Marcia sought biblically-based educational and training programs that had already proven to be effective in each area to be addressed. They then entered into licensing agreements with the facilitating ministries, personally paid to have the materials translated into Portuguese (the language of Brazil), and recruited and trained volunteers and staff to implement the programs. From this, the University of the Family was born.

University of the Family

Between 1992 and 2014, over one million people participated in University of the Family's courses across the country, approximately half a percent of Brazil's population. By the close of 2017, more than 10,000 groups had participated in family enrichment training throughout Brazil.

University of the Family is focused on supporting, empowering, and resourcing churches throughout Brazil to help them strengthen families in all aspects of their lives. Jorge said churches often don't know how to tackle the areas of family ministry addressed by University of the Family because they lack the ability to connect their congregants, train leaders, or produce or pay for the materials. But if a church agrees to participate, he says, they take ownership by sponsoring the programs, and with the help of the pastor, they identify and recruit up to 20 potential leader couples per training session. University of the Family trains the leaders to use their small-group methodology and materials. Small groups are favored because they provide an environment of intimacy, sharing, bonding, and support. A strategic byproduct for the church is that people who go through University of the Family's training programs become the church's future leaders. Churches that have adopted University of the Family's programs have seen their congregations mature spiritually, become more vibrant and participatory, and increase regular service attendance.

Currently, the five primary program ministries of the University of the Family are as follows.

Family Foundations International

This is a Christian ministry dedicated to helping individuals, couples, and families become people of influence and to build a godly heritage for multiple generations by restoring biblical foundations of marriage, family, and finance.

Growing Families International

This is a global community of parents linked together by common biblical values, beliefs, and noble outcomes. Its purpose is to create a positive culture of parenting in which mothers and fathers feel informed, appreciated, and empowered; and their children feel safe, valued, and loved.

Crown Financial Ministries

Its mission is to advance transformation by equipping servant leaders to live by God's design for their finances, work, and life. It provides extensive resources and training for all ages and groups to learn how to discover and live their God-given purpose and to manage their resources according to biblical principles.

Christian Men's Network

This is a highly effective global movement of pastors and leaders dedicated to training men to fulfill their roles as servant leaders for their family, church, and culture. This is University of the Family's largest growth area. "If the husband-father becomes a Christian," Jorge says, "eighty percent of the family comes along."

Growing Leaders

This organization helps to prepare tomorrow's leaders today through effective, customizable youth and student leadership development programs. Its unique events and scripturally-based resources are focused on creating a healthy culture that fosters leadership at all levels, giving adults the tools they need to connect with the emerging generation, guiding unprepared teens to productive adulthood and equipping students to think and act like authentic leaders.

In 2017, University of the Family had 70 paid staff members, over 10,000 volunteers and leaders, and served over 105,000 people per year through more than 1,500 churches. The ministry expects to reach the next one million participants in seven to eight years and then sustain a growth rate thereafter of one million people served in Brazil every four to five years. The growth is accomplished by the leaders trained each year at University of the Family. In 2016, over 300 leader-training programs were conducted, and 30 to 50 leaders were trained in each session—about 12,000 leaders trained in all.

Jorge and Marcia made the initial capital contributions to get the ministry going, but from the beginning, University of the Family was designed and intended to be self-sustaining. Operational revenue is provided through a small markup on the cost of the materials provided to leaders and participants. The small groups also typically take offerings and make donations to University of the Family. All of the revenue received is used to cover ministry expenses. Jorge and Marcia do not receive any compensation.

Jorge and his family are also putting his seven-mountain ecosystem beliefs to the test in Pompéia. The hope is to build a model for bringing together the seven mountains of influence in any community anywhere in the world. Pompéia is called the "city of heart, hospitality, generosity, and love" and is looked upon as one of the best cities in Brazil. This is undoubtedly in part because one of the nation's best companies is headquartered there and has heavily invested in the area and its people. Jorge said,

> Pompéia may seem too small to make a difference. It is a rural farming community of about 20,000. But we have made a difference here, and we can do likewise for other communities with our leadership and example. The highest level of leadership is connecting all of the mountains of influence.

Oasis Community Center for Kids

The Nishimura family links arts and entertainment to the other six mountains of influence in Pompéia through the Oasis Community Center for Kids. Underwritten by proceeds from brother Lincoln's life-insurance policy in his memory, Oasis houses and funds 127 arts-and-entertainment programs and 56 sports programs that touch over 1,500 kids in the community and in the 10 public schools it serves.

The Oasis facility is impressive: clean and intricately planned with soundproof music rooms for practice and instruction, art rooms, a spacious and well-equipped dance practice area, sports fields and facilities, and various other areas for kids of all ages to learn and develop. The students perform throughout the community; create video presentations; and engage their parents, peers, friends, and teachers in their activities. The Oasis kids interact with energy, joy, and mutual respect; are excited about learning; and are growing in confidence and self-esteem. Their life-giving joy is cultivated in their socially and spiritually flourishing community.

Enterprise Family Responsible

As of the close of 2017, Jorge was in the process of building Enterprise Family Responsible, a model to expand the work of strengthening families by leveraging the work and resources of University of the Family with area employers to reach people who do not attend church. The programs are secular but are based on biblical principles, bringing God into the conversation. The goal is to expand the model throughout Brazil by encouraging and training companies to provide educational and self-improvement tracks for their employees. Jorge believes an employee who is happier at home is almost always more productive at work. In 2017, more than 1,500 people went through the program, and the numbers are growing every year.

Jorge is also creating a reproduceable model to get entire communities more deeply involved in improving their public schools. This model will create a road map for how to get parents more involved in improving campus facilities and bring business, government, and church leaders of the city together to develop and execute a 20-year vision for providing superior education. The results will be mutually beneficial for students, families, and communities as well as for the local employers through improved quality of their future employees. That model will be built, tested, and readied for wider distribution in Pompéia.

Bumpuku: "Happiness in Sharing"

Why do Jorge and the Nishimura family push so hard to grow and continue their business, to strengthen their family ties, and to make sure their family and business give back in a myriad of ways? It all comes down to *bumpuku*, a Japanese word that translates to "happiness in sharing," the last of Jacto's 10 core values. For the Nishimura family, it is their most important and all-encompassing value. It started with Shunji, continues through Jorge and his siblings, and has taken root with the third generation. There is unison around the family's dedication to ensure that *bumpuku* will continue to be part of their legacy to future generations. Jorge said,

> We seek to have relevance in what we do. We always want to do more. Our family enjoys serving and helping others. This was instilled in us by our parents. There is pleasure in our service. These common points give us harmony with each other and with God. Selfish behavior destroys family unity. Our shared service is our pleasure and our glue. It adds value to our family.

He added that the root word of *bumpuku* in Japanese means "equivalent of tithe" and that, according to Scripture, to tithe is to give the best, our first fruits (Exodus 23:19).

> First fruits are whatever it is we have to give. To give first fruits is not to give a number or percentage. Rather, it is to recognize that everything good comes from God, that we are His stewards, and that we honor and glorify Him by giving back the first and very best of that which He has already bestowed upon us.
>
> We are regularly confronted with a choice: to serve God or to serve ourselves. How we respond to this choice reveals our hearts and, therefore, our motives. Our choice reflects whether or not we truly love God with all of our heart, soul, mind, and strength. We can give the very best of our time, our abilities, and our resources back to God in His service, or we can use it for ourselves.

Jorge believes this responsibility of stewardship includes the businesses they oversee. Alluding to 2 Corinthians 9:6-15, he said,

> It is imperative to ask if we have committed ourselves as stewards of the business that God has given us to manage. When we give with open hands and open, pure hearts, we experience the great joy proclaimed in the Bible.

It's not a surprise that the most prominent piece of art in Jorge's office is a rendering given to him by a dear friend that depicts Christ on His knees washing the feet of His disciples. It all adds up to *bumpuku*, happiness in sharing the first and very best of all that God has provided for him and his family. Jorge said,

> My expression of love for God is in my service. This is my joy. If it were all about keeping the money or accumulating things, I would be miserable. Serving others for God is something I do with pleasure and passion.

Personal Reflection and Group Discussion

1. Do you have a list of personal core values? Using Jorge's examples, create five core values that are your non-negotiable rules of behavior that you hold sacred.

2. Jorge said, "We are regularly confronted with a choice to serve God or to serve ourselves." How does your response to this choice reveal your heart and motives?

3. What are you doing to grow the next generation of leaders in your company? Who can help you accelerate your progress in this area?

4. Shortly after Jorge had opened his heart and his hands to God, he was fired by his family. He was shocked and bewildered with why God would allow this to happen. Can you identify times when you wondered why God was allowing difficulties to happen to you—yet, like Jorge, you can see in hindsight that God was using the situation to align you with His plan for your life?

5. Brazil is a country ripe with corruption. Jorge and Jacto have no tolerance for corruption. Jorge stated that not compromising their biblical principles and values is more important than money. Where do you draw the line regarding not compromising biblical principles and values?

6. What other spiritual, business, and personal concepts and practices noted in this chapter stood out to you? How will you integrate them into your life and/or business?

4

CONTENTMENT? YES ... AND NO:
BARNHART CRANE AND RIGGING

Memphis, TN, USA

ALAN AND KATHERINE BARNHART BEGAN THEIR JOURNEY to find contentment after they became engaged. Alan had earned a degree in civil engineering from the University of Tennessee, and the couple decided to be missionaries in a country in the heart of the Middle East. Foreign civil engineers were in great demand during the 1980s when the country they selected was expanding its oil and gas production infrastructure. Alan's engineering work provided temporary residence status there even though it was a country typically closed to missionaries. Katherine was thrilled because she had always dreamed of engaging in mission work overseas. Their plan was to move in 1986, a year after their wedding day, and then network with their Muslim neighbors and quietly witness to them about Christianity. Alan and Katherine were excited! They felt that God had paved the way for their future ministry.

Then, everything changed. Alan's parents decided to retire from the business they had founded and built in Memphis, Tennessee, Barnhart Construction Company, and circumnavigate the globe on their sailboat. If Alan and his brother Eric—who both had been working in the company since they were children—decided not to purchase it, his parents were going to sell the business to a third party.

Katherine hoped Alan wanted to forge ahead with their plans to work and live in the Middle East. She was convinced they'd be doing something significant with their lives by being missionaries there. Alan hesitated, believing that God had given him a passion and a purpose to use his civil engineering degree in business. He felt God was drawing him to the family business. Alan was confident he could serve God's will and still be in mission work through Barnhart Construction Company.

A young woman with deep faith, Katherine wanted to support her new husband. Knowing Alan's motives were Christ-centered, prayerful, and pure, Katherine felt compelled to submit to his wishes even though it meant the end of her dream of overseas mission work.

Alan and Eric created a new entity—Barnhart Crane and Rigging—hired the 10 existing employees from Barnhart Construction Company, and continued working with the same clients. They rented the equipment from their parents and ultimately purchased it.

Serving as Faithful Stewards

Alan set to work with his brother Eric—with an attitude of caution. Both were aware that earthly success can lead to spiritual failure, so before they went into business together, they decided that everything they had belonged to God and that it was to be His company. They were going to strive to serve Him as faithful stewards.

To protect themselves from what they considered to be the dangers of wealth, they set what they referred to as a "financial finish line." This was of critical importance to Alan as, several years prior, he had meticulously studied every verse in the Bible related to money and wealth and had written and ordered them for future reference. Alan saw the warnings throughout Scripture that wealth can get in the way of a relationship with God. He was particularly convicted by Jesus' blunt statement that people cannot serve both God and money (Matthew 6:24).

Three other Bible verses took residence in Alan's mind and pierced his heart. One was Luke 12:15 in which Jesus said,

> Watch out! Be on your guard against all kinds of greed; life does not consist in an abundance of possessions.

The second was 1 Timothy 6:9-10:

> Those who want to get rich fall into temptation and a trap and into many foolish and harmful desires that plunge people into ruin and destruction. For the love of money is a root of all kinds of evil. Some people, eager for money, have wandered from the faith and pierced themselves with many griefs.

Alan observed that these passages teach that

> ...money itself isn't bad because money is a tool given by God that can be powerfully used to help people. But rather, it is the love of money and how it can be used in a self-serving manner that is destructive.

It was the third verse, however, Colossians 3:23-34, that helped Alan get excited about building and growing a business and even maximizing its profit.

> Whatever you do, work at it with all your heart, as working for the Lord, not for human masters, since you know that you will receive an inheritance from

the Lord as a reward. It is the Lord Christ you are serving.

Alan realized that it was his heart and his motives that were most important to God.

Alan and Eric agreed upon a financial finish line to 1) cap their income at that of the middle-income members of their adult Sunday school class, 2) use 50 percent of the profit to fund ministry work, and 3) invest the remainder of the profit in the people and resources necessary to grow Barnhart.

One evening, Alan, Eric, and their wives gathered to pray to entrust their new business to God and commit to their financial finish line. Alan was at peace about the direction they chose. He and Eric then told a few friends and people at work about their commitment.

> That locked in our decision and gave us some real accountability. We set out not to get rich personally in financial terms. We set out to avoid getting rich. The opportunity we had, after all, was one that God had graciously given to us, and we were determined to be good and faithful stewards, keeping our motives pure.

"Profit with a Purpose"

Barnhart Crane and Rigging is not your typical crane company involved in commercial building construction. It specializes in lifting, rigging, and transporting extremely heavy and unwieldy objects—typically, huge industrial components. Barnhart has transported and placed mechanisms like massive wind turbines, enormous power-plant transformers, a launchpad structural support for NASA, a 700-ton furnace, and a 1,800-ton industrial precipitator. You've likely seen one of Barnhart's placements, the scoreboard above the field at the Dallas Cowboys' football stadium in Arlington, Texas, one of the world's largest LED TV monitors.

Barnhart's tagline is "Minds Over Matter," and it has built a nationwide reputation for solving unique and highly complex problems through its 60 engineers who work with real-life erector sets. Its specialty cranes and transportation rigs are highly engineered, innovative, and use a large amount of hydraulics.

Alan and Eric grew up around the business because the company's headquarters was two bedrooms of the family's home in its first 17 years of existence. The brothers started working in the company as children and never stopped. Both were employed as iron workers and crane operators throughout high school and college. When the brothers started running the business in 1986, Barnhart had ten employees and eight cranes, and they immediately launched their "Profit with a Purpose" commitment:

> Barnhart will attempt to make a profit and will invest the profit to expand the company and meet the needs of people (physically, mentally, and spiritually).

Alan and Eric decided to be equal shareholders of the business and agreed to strive to work for the Lord and build a business that glorified Him in every way. It was what they did with the fruit of their labor that was going to define their success and joy in life.

It didn't take long for their plan to take root. By the end of their first year in business in 1986, they gave away $50,000, more than either of their salaries. The brothers were ecstatic, and both were comfortable with the roles they played in the company. "Eric is a mechanical genius," Alan said, "but he admittedly is not wired to run a business." Therefore, Alan took the leadership role while Eric contributed his immense and valuable mechanical skills, allowing both the freedom to do what they do best and enjoy most to serve the company.

They also quickly recognized that they needed help to relieve themselves from their 100-hour work weeks to take the business to the next level. They decided to seek and hire some "right fit," highly-talented professionals who could propel the business' growth. The "Profit with a Purpose" commitment became a valuable tool to help prospective employees understand the Barnhart culture, and for some, it was a drawing card. Of those hired between 1987 and 2000, Alan reports that several key people remain in leadership positions today.

Hinge Points

The company has experienced key "hinge points" over the years around which the company turned—some good and others difficult. Yet because Alan and Eric always turned to God for direction and clarity and had always seen themselves as servant stewards and not owners, even the difficulties have contributed to the long-term success of the company.

The first hinge point was when the boom-or-bust oil and gas industry went into a "bust" phase in 1986, and Barnhart was able to purchase cranes at auction at substantial discounts. This enabled them to reduce the large capital expenses typically required to grow a company dependent on expensive equipment, and as a result, they quickly increased Barnhart's bottom-line profit.

The second hinge point was in 1991 when Barnhart was able to buy out an aggressive local competitor in Memphis. Their bottom-line profit immediately increased as they won more business and made a reasonable profit from those contracts.

The third one occurred in 1992 when a talented team member posed the idea to open a branch location to expand the business. Barnhart was making enough money to expand its geographic footprint, so it decided to take the employee up on his proposal and opened their first branch in Decatur, Alabama. Shortly thereafter, Barnhart initiated a strategy to grow by creating full-service branches of the company in other cities. Branches were then strategically added in locations around the country that were within Barnhart's target markets. Some branches were added through opportunistic acquisitions of local companies; others were added for proven team members who wanted to relocate to a specific city and run a branch operation.

Alan liked growing through decentralization. He prefers finding capable people who have the right values, fit the company culture, and are motivated to work hard and contribute to the company's success. However, Alan learned that there had to be a clear delineation of responsibilities and authority to be successful with a decentralized approach, with strong accountability measures put in place to ensure he had the right people leading the branches. Over time, Barnhart initiated and refined the following processes and programs to ensure the success of the decentralized branches.

All administrative functions such as accounting, banking, and insurance are handled at the home office in Memphis. This fosters companywide efficiency and cost reduction in administrative functions while allowing branch managers freedom to focus on their business without being distracted by administrative duties and issues.

Branch managers are allowed a great deal of latitude in their decision-making. They develop their own leadership teams and succession plans and determine their areas of focus for sales and marketing. They choose their fleet and equipment from a home-office "menu" and have flexibility in how they invest profit back into their businesses. They are also allowed to negotiate their own contracts. The home office does, however, have to sign off on every contract before it can be executed.

Safety measures are mandated by the home office, and safety is known to be one of the top priorities at Barnhart.

Strong accountability is essential to keeping everyone in the company working in unison toward the same short-term and long-term objectives and to protect the company culture. Alan said,

> Part of our company's "secret sauce" that makes decentralization successful is the measurements utilized in the Branch Scorecard process in combination with our self-managing culture.

In this process, he said each branch's performance is closely evaluated on a regular basis using a number of measures. The primary financial measurements are the branch's return on capital and growth of profit.

Today, Barnhart has 47 branches and over 1,100 employees throughout the United States, and its expertise is sought by those around the globe who have unique and challenging jobs.

Knocked to His Knees

By the late 1990s, Barnhart was well positioned to take advantage of a big boom in the installation of gas turbines needed for electricity production, which lasted until the terrorist attacks of September 11, 2001. But as it grew dramatically, adding the cranes and people required to take advantage of this new business, the expansion was marred by a marked increase in accidents. Alan said,

> We had some people make big mistakes that caused bad things to happen... accidents where big and expensive pieces of equipment were damaged or destroyed.

It was a terribly trying time, and as Alan's confidence was shaken, he was knocked to his knees in prayer. He struggled with what he and the company could have done differently to prevent the accidents. Alan also feared for the ongoing viability of the company, so much so that it seemed like everything was going to implode. He said,

> Through a lot of prayer, I found peace that it is all in God's hands, and if He wanted me elsewhere, that was His call. My job was to do my best to follow His will as I led the company, and the rest was up to Him.

He knew he, his family, and his employees were going to be fine no matter what God decided.

> God also helped me realize that I could not let our problems ruin the organization by overreacting. I perceived that it was imperative for me to balance my response and react with a steadying hand and strong leadership when things go bad.

Alan felt led by the Lord to focus on the problems and how to use what he learned to make sure the company never had those types of issues again.

> We hired an expert to help us develop and imple-ment vastly improved safety protocols, procedures, and accountability processes. Our safety record im-mediately began to improve and has been excellent ever since. There is no telling how many injuries or even deaths have been prevented and equipment protected as a result of allowing God to lead us through that dark time. I learned once again that worry is counterproductive. When you have God's peace, you can focus on the appropriate solutions.

The Leadership Team

Another significant hinge point occurred in 2002 when Alan assembled a senior leadership team. It consisted of leaders that Alan trusted for their integrity, intelligence, and dedication to the company's culture. The first project of the newly organized team was to document the company's purpose, mission, and core values. Their collaboration produced the following:

> **Purpose Statement**: The purpose of Barnhart Crane and Rigging is to glorify God by providing an opportunity for His people to use their skills and gifts in His service through constructive work, personal witness, and ministry funding.

> **Mission Statement**: Barnhart will continuously improve and grow to be the best heavy-lift and heavy-transport company.

> **Core Values**: Safety, Quality Service, Innovation, Continuous Improvement, Fairness, and Profit with a Purpose

The leadership team was also charged with creating a never-ending process to improve the company's safety record continually. They instituted a heightened companywide focus on safety. By elevating safety to one of their core values and, therefore, part of the lifeblood of the organization, the company currently experiences one-eighth of the incidents that it did in 2002.

The senior leadership team now meets weekly to maintain accountability to their commitments, measure progress, and solve problems. Additionally, they invest two to three days each quarter and one week each year in off-site meetings to ensure they are continually refocusing and coordinating their efforts. To achieve long-term success, the senior leadership team realized that innovation had to be one of the company's core competencies. They decided that, because every job is unique, they had to create more efficient and effective methods to safely do the jobs and increase profitability. Eric and his team of problem-solving engineers designed and built lifting equipment and techniques not available to other companies. These innovations give Barnhart a significant competitive advantage in their target markets.

Another priority of Barnhart is getting the right people in the right job. Alan said,

> At the executive level, finding the right people whose life-thinking aligns with our culture is one of the keys to the success of our company. This doesn't mean everyone has the same theology. We want and need different personalities and talent, but where we need everyone on the same page is with their life-thinking—or, personal values. Finding and keeping key guys who align with our culture is also one of our most daunting challenges. When we do make a mistake in hiring, quickly recognizing that someone doesn't fit is imperative. There is a lot of pain in keeping the wrong person.

Not surprisingly, hiring the right people trickles down to their ground-level workers as well.

> We find and hire lots of good, hard-working people who excel at what they do. We have made mistakes but have learned and improved from them as a result. We know that we have to hire someone for their character first and then their talent.

Once someone is hired, Barnhart constantly reevaluates how to place the best people in the jobs most suited for their skills.

> We are also quick to let someone go if they don't fit our culture. We see it as helping the employee get in a better place.

The senior leadership team faced new challenges following 9/11 and the subsequent failure of the Enron Company. The gas turbine business went from 50 percent of Barnhart's revenue to five percent, and for the next four years, Barnhart scrambled to make up the lost revenue. They were able to remain profitable, and the leadership team used what they had learned during this difficult time to realign their business plan so they could build on the remaining base of business and resume Barnhart's growth.

> Looking back, I see that time period as an important "hinge point" in which we could have succumbed to the difficult times. Instead, we chose to see it as an opportunity to improve our business model and rise to the challenges at hand.

Fueling Growth

Part of the base-building process was a decision to not rely heavily on long-term debt to fuel the company's growth. While Barnhart is a capital-intensive business that requires the acquisition of expensive equipment and continues to grow, in part, through the acquisition of other companies, Barnhart continues to maintain a debt-to-equity ratio range well below the industry average. This low ratio gives Barnhart the financial freedom to think long-term and to innovate in ways that other companies that carry much higher debt cannot consider.

Barnhart's innovation-minded executives also find niches where they can solve problems, provide value, and be profitable.

In 2003, the company was asked to bid on a job to install 80 wind turbines in Wyoming. Barnhart had never done a wind farm installation, wind turbines are complicated and difficult to set up, and Barnhart didn't have a branch office within 1,500 miles. The leadership team had many reasons to decline placing a bid. But "we are can-do guys," Alan said. "And we got the job. It was 'all hands on deck' to figure out the best way to do the job." They found a way, the project went well, and the manufacturer loved the work.

The next year, Barnhart took another wind farm installation job in Knoxville, Tennessee but ended up losing money on the contract. At a crossroads of choosing either to exit the wind business before potentially losing more money or seeking to get a return on investment on the knowledge they had amassed, Barnhart opted to try two more wind farm jobs. The decision paid off. From 2005-2008, the company's revenue grew from $50 million to $250 million. In 2008, $100 million came from wind farm contracts.

Of course, the decision of when to reduce or exit certain market opportunities can be just as important as the decision to get into and invest in that business segment. In 2009, the Barnhart leadership team chose to decrease its wind farm business methodically, disbanding the division dedicated to wind at the end of 2012. The wind farm segment now accounts for about 15 percent of the company's revenue. While the top-line revenue of the wind business has dissipated significantly, the bottom line profit actually grew as they accepted only jobs with the most profit potential.

In that same year of 2012, Barnhart implemented a training program to identify and assimilate more quickly the best entry-level employees into the business. The program, called "Lifting and Transportation Trainee," is a two-year "up or out" program in which trainees are paid a modest hourly wage and are expected to work hard and learn by doing. If the trainee sticks with the program, by the end of two years, both the company and the trainee know they have a good fit. Because the program was introduced via the internet, hundreds of people have applied. Barnhart has now graduated approximately 60 trainees at the time of this writing, which makes up almost five percent of its workforce. Alan said,

> We have hired some great guys, including guys with degrees and even engineers. Our results have been outstanding, and our branches have signed up. As our people get better, so does our future.

Army Cooks

Eric and Alan have always believed that the army cook shouldn't eat any better than the troops, and they apply this philosophy to themselves in their company. They knew it was essential if they were to honor their financial finish line. As a result, Alan and Eric are paid exactly the same salary as every member of the senior leadership team. Bonuses can also be earned and vary based upon each executive's objectives and accomplishments. Each year, it is not uncommon at Barnhart for some executives to receive more total compensation than Alan or Eric. Barnhart also provides a deferred compensation plan in which the company's executives vest after 15 years of employment. The plan will significantly, if not fully, continue the executive's compensation at retirement. Many of the more seasoned executives today are fully vested yet choose to continue working at Barnhart because they love the challenges and the culture.

In the 30-plus years since they took over the company under the "army cook" model, Alan, Eric, and their team have grown Barnhart's revenue to over $300 million. Most importantly to them, however, they have kept their financial finish line commitment. As the company grew, so did the amount they were able to give to various ministries and charities—from $50,000 the first year to more than $1 million per month by 2005. By 2018, the cumulative amount given had grown to well over $100 million, and Barnhart was giving away over $1.5 million per month.

Giving It Away

From the beginning of their venture together, Alan and Katherine created and then refined the GROVE process to overcome what Alan described as "our biggest challenge: figuring out how to give the money away the right way." GROVE is an acronym for "God's Resources Operating Very Effectively." The GROVE Group has its own vision, mission, and values statements. It also has a detailed business plan regarding the types of organizations GROVE will contribute to and how it will make the donations. GROVE was built on a foundation that contains the following primary philosophies:

- Never do for others what they can do for themselves.
- Never give in a manner that creates dependence. This hurts the receiver and the giver.
- Don't cross barriers where you don't know how the money is going to be used and/or where there is not a system for accountability.
- Give through indigenous ministries wherever possible, providing them with the boost necessary to lift themselves and become self-sustaining.

To receive a grant, a ministry must have a Barnhart employee or employee's spouse as its "ministry champion." Champions are responsible for researching and building a relationship with the ministry, making funding recommendations, and then working with the ministry and reporting to the GROVE board and project review committee what the ministry has accomplished with the funds. To become a champion, an employee or an employee's spouse must apply for the position and then go through an interview and training process. The GROVE board has also created a process to match their champions with a ministry for which the champion can be passionate about serving.

The GROVE Group has a 10-member board of directors, six of whom are on the project review committee. The GROVE Group also has many champions. The project review committee meets monthly and reviews and approves grant proposals under $100,000 as well as champions' assessment trips. The board meets quarterly and reviews and approves grants over $100,000. They also make decisions about GROVE policies and procedures.

GROVE has about 100 different ministry partners at any given point that are located around the globe. There is no budget. Instead, they have the immense responsibility of giving away 100 percent of the yearly Barnhart profits not reinvested in company growth in a manner that will accomplish the GROVE Group's vision to "seek to advance the kingdom of God through the effective funding of strategic ministry throughout the world." The GROVE Group's mission and values statements add clarity and structure to this vision statement.

Estate Planning

As the company grew, Alan and Eric knew they needed to make some decisions about the company's longevity and who would own it following their respective deaths. They knew they wanted the company and its giving to continue, so in 2007, they began working to formalize estate plans and a business continuation plan for themselves and for Barnhart. They found traditional strategies to be cumbersome and expensive; therefore, against the advice of some of the professionals whose counsel they sought, they decided to explore giving the entire company away to charity.

Alan reached out to Terry Parker with the National Christian Foundation (NCF) to seek a solution. Terry and the experts at NCF were instrumental in helping the Barnharts craft and implement a plan that accomplished their objectives. Alan and Eric agreed not to keep the company or transfer it to their heirs but, instead, to divest themselves and fully give the company to God's ministry. Though Alan still runs the company and Eric continues his engineering work, in 2007, they transferred their stock in the company to two trusts of which the beneficiary is a qualified charitable Donor Advised Fund administrated by the NCF that is named the GROVE Group Fund. A donor-advised fund is a charitable giving vehicle sponsored by an IRS-qualified public charity that allows the donor to contribute to that charity and be eligible for an immediate tax deduction, and then recommend grants over time to any other IRS-qualified public charity. Neither the Barnharts nor their heirs will ever benefit financially from the company's growing value. If a family member wants to work in the business, he or she will be paid the same amount as a non-family coworker performing the same duties.

One trust was established as the owner of 99 percent of Barnhart's non-voting stock, and another trust was designated as the owner of the remaining one percent of voting stock. Alan was designated as the trustee of the voting trust to vote on behalf of the company and its employees. If Alan were to become no longer able or willing to serve as trustee in the best interest of the company, the trust's board of advisors are responsible for replacing him. The trust ensures that Barnhart continues as an operating company so it can continue to be the economic engine for the GROVE Group's giving. If the company is ever sold, the proceeds will be distributed by the trusts to the GROVE Group

Donor Advised Fund at NCF to be distributed to ministries and charities according to their guidelines.

Succession Planning

In order to continue the company, its growth, and its giving into the future, Barnhart needed a solid leadership succession plan. Accordingly, the company's board of advisors is charged with always keeping the right CEO at the helm. Clear, written guidelines are in place for the company's board that emphasize the CEO is to be a committed steward in addition to being a great leader. Alan believes the two together are much more powerful than either one individually. He said,

> I don't see running the business as a distraction from my ministry; it *is* my ministry! When financials come out, I'm very interested to see how we are doing and if we are making money. Some people might look askance at that, but I want us to push hard and be good at what we do according to biblical principles.
>
> We believe that doing good work through rigging projects is ministry, and we bring glory to God by how we go about our work using God's scriptural principles. And, by bringing our resources to new places, we extend our ministry and our reach. The company also provides the fuel to empower the ministries in which we invest our profit.

While it might seem counterintuitive, the company has continued to grow at a rate of 18 percent per year since the two trusts and the NCF GROVE Group fund became the beneficiary. Senior leadership team member Matt Brennan who started with Barnhart in 2009 said,

When I came to work here, the fact that the company was owned by the trusts, and ultimately the NCF fund, was a positive for me. It exhibited that the company's purpose and mission were more than just words, and I knew that the company could not be sold out from under us. It gave me the comfort that there is a bigger reason for the company to continue. I was confident that I could make a long-term investment in my career at Barnhart and be in ministry at the same time. Since I started here, I have come to really appreciate getting to work hard on a project, help the company earn a fair profit, and then be able to help give that profit away to a kingdom-building ministry as a GROVE ministry champion.

In addition to Alan being deeply engaged in the success of the company and the ministries it supports, Matt believes the empowerment given by Alan to the leadership team is a reason why Barnhart continues to thrive.

We were given the responsibility and have helped create a plan and structure that will successfully continue our company into the future. The goal is to have our company and our culture long outlive Alan. I don't believe that there are Christian companies, just Christians working in companies guided by biblical principles. For a company to be first class, you have to put the purpose first. Being a Christian is not required, but everyone is aware of the purpose when they come on board. Hopefully, they will come to appreciate our faith by the way we live and work together.

Alan revealed that he was gratified, yet also somewhat surprised, by the change in attitude when the company was given away.

> When Eric and I were the sole owners, the future was never 100 percent clear for the leadership team. I believe they trusted me, but there was always a possibility that my motives, or those of my heirs, could change. With the company owned by the foundation, there is clarity about the motives—the driving force for our company, the company's future, and the leadership succession. Because the entire company has been given away, they also know that Katherine's and my lifestyle will always be based on what we earn through the company—just like them. And, because the company's priority is to give away everything not reinvested back into the company for growth, they know that our compensation will always be maintained at a modest level. The structure is in place to support all of us working together in unison toward the same purpose.

Additionally, Alan said the change in ownership communicated the intention to keep God at the center of the business. He is convinced that this "God factor" enhances their business and work environment in many ways.

> It changes how you relate to and treat people. Everyone, faith or no faith, appreciates being treated with loving care and respect. It also drives you to provide a productive and safe work environment and an opportunity for your employees to earn, grow, and participate in excellent company benefits.

God has also provided for Barnhart in ways Alan said it could never have accomplished on its own.

> A great example is we were presented, out of the blue, with an opportunity to purchase an old Army depot in Memphis when the government decided to divest themselves of the property. We bought it at a very deep discount and it opened up a new source of substantial revenue for us using portions of the vast property and the accompanying warehouses to store industrial equipment for other companies. Another example is how God is able to use our business to get us into countries and spread the gospel that we could never get into through traditional ministry channels. Miracles do happen when God is at the center of your purpose!

Alan reported that he and his team are not shy about referencing Bible verses at company meetings when it relates to the topic at hand. In addition, he said,

> We also recognize and honor companywide the Christian celebrations of Christmas, Easter, and Thanksgiving. We constantly look for ways to serve God that we would not consider if our business was not our ministry.

Barnhart created a ministry for ex-convicts called Economic Opportunities that provides care and training to get them started in the workplace after they have been released from incarceration.

> They have the chance to learn a skill, prove themselves as employees, and become employable. After a year, they move on to another job. Their labor

helps reduce our cost in supporting the ministry, and Barnhart is able to help them get back on their feet and in a position to contribute to society.

Remaining Focused

Even with God at the center of their business, Alan understands that, in order to help the company continue to grow, he must keep his leadership team engaged. He does this by making sure they are intentionally focusing on and developing capabilities for the right business segments and customers, pricing correctly, providing great project management, innovating in all areas of operations and administration, and doing what he calls "the blocking and tackling" (i.e. fundamentals) of running and administrating the company properly. He said,

> Passion alone doesn't matter. You have to *do* something with that passion that is productive toward God's purpose for your life.

Alan also knows that, to help Barnhart fulfill its purpose, he must prioritize his limited and valuable time to remain in close and constant relationship with the Lord. In addition to praying throughout the day, he dedicates significant time—usually in the morning—to reading the Bible and praying, seeking God's will, praising the Lord, and thanking Him for His blessings. He uses this time to seek and understand God's purposes for him. To emphasize why this time is so important to him, he quoted John 10:10, Jesus' words in reference to Satan: "The thief comes only to steal and kill and destroy; I have come that they may have life, and have it to the full." He explained,

> God's abundant life is fun, interesting, and exciting! When we are obedient, we make progress and help others, which is life-giving. Making daily progress

in my faith and helping others has provided a massive dose of abundant life for me. I think that is how God intended it—that we have our entire life bound together as one: spiritually, in business, and our personal life.

What became of Katherine's desire to be in overseas missions work? It has been more than realized through the dynamic ministry that Barnhart Rigging and Crane has become and through the GROVE giving process in which she has been intimately involved. As observed in the spring 2014 issue of *Philanthropy* magazine,

> The Barnhart kids didn't get trips to Disney World, or even treats at the grocery store. Instead, their parents took them to developing countries to see the wells, churches, and farms their gifts had enabled.[2]

Alan said,

> Always striving to be good and faithful stewards and purposefully grow our business and its ability to increase our GROVE Group giving is so much more fulfilling than accumulating or consuming. Katherine and I are completely content with what we have, but Barnhart will never be satisfied with maintaining the status quo. We believe we always need to push to do more to serve God through our work and our giving.

Striving as trusting and faithful stewards. Growing God's business. Happiness through purposefully giving back to God the fruit of their labor. Joy through service to God and others. This is how Alan and Katherine Barnhart have personally realized and pass on contentment—and why Alan and the leaders of Barnhart will never be completely content.

Author's note: *Alan shared with a smile and in the spirit of full disclosure that, following the publication of the quote in Philanthropy magazine, a pastor he met and befriended at a conference invited Alan, Katherine, and their two youngest children to visit him and his family at his home in Orlando. The Barnharts accepted, and you can probably guess the rest of the story. The pastor treated them to an excursion to Disney World, a special indulgence for all!*

Personal Reflection and Group Discussion

1. Alan and Eric were acutely aware that earthly success can lead to spiritual failure and, from the beginning, decided that everything they had belonged to God and that Barnhart was to be God's company. What do you think about Jesus' and Paul's warnings about money in Luke 12:15 and 1 Timothy 6:9-10, respectively? Like Alan, can the wisdom found in Colossians 3:23-24 help you get excited about maximizing your company's profit?

2. Instead of succumbing to the problems and pressures that resulted from their safety failures, Barnhart's senior leadership team used what they learned to leap into action to correct the problems and put themselves in a better position to grow safely. Alan explained, "Through a lot of prayer, I found peace that it is all God's and, if He wanted me elsewhere, that was His call. My job was to do my best to follow His will as I led the company, and the rest was up to Him." Have you ever had a situation where God helped you navigate through overwhelming problems instead of succumbing to them? What did you learn from that experience?

3. As their company grew, so did the Barnhart's giving to various ministries through the GROVE process. Examine your giving to God's work. Does anything need to change? Are there takeaways from the GROVE process that you can implement in your company?

4. Alan said of Barnhart, "We believe we always need to push to do more to serve God through our work and our giving." How can you strive to be more content with what you have yet never completely content with what you give in your service to God?

5. What other spiritual, business, and personal concepts and practices noted in this chapter stood out to you? How will you integrate them into your life and/or business?

5

HEALING HEARTS:
AMAHORO AVA HEJURU
COOPERATIVE

Kigali, Rwanda

GRACE NYIRABARINDA SAT IN SILENCE among a handful of women in the market where they sewed clothing, handbags, napkins, and other items to sell each day. Grace was there because her sister-in-law feared Grace was going to kill herself and hoped the sewing ladies could help her.

But what can they do for me? Grace pondered as she stood looking downward, unwilling to make eye contact with anyone. Grace knew it would have been much simpler had her problems been physical, but it was her heart that was lost, along with every last ounce of her faith and hope. Now, only hatred, bitterness, anger, and sadness remained; the combination tormented her to the point of despair.

Grace briefly glanced at her sister-in-law, appreciative of her compassionate act of bringing her to the market. These impoverished women didn't know her story, but Grace assumed her sister-in-law had chosen them because they surely understood her pain. Each one of them had experienced their own trauma and heartbreak as a result of the 1994 genocide in Rwanda. Despite her silence, the women began sharing with

Grace what they had already shared with one another—compassion and love. They did this by reading the Bible and praying together, and Grace marveled as these hurting women sang hymns as they sewed by hand and on their pedal-powered machines.

Hesitantly at first, but then with growing interest, Grace also allowed them to teach her to sew. Grace returned regularly to the marketplace, joined the sewing group, and came to trust these women because they truly cared for her. She felt secure in their company. Stitch by agonizing stitch, she unfolded her story to them.

The Genocide

Between April 6 and July 15, 1994, approximately one million Tutsi men, women, and children and moderate Hutu Rwandan people sympathetic to the Tutsi's safety were brutally tortured, raped, and murdered in a well-planned and organized genocidal effort by extreme Hutu nationalists. The hostility that led to these atrocities dated back to 1959 when the majority Hutus initiated a civil war to drive the minority Tutsi people from Rwanda to eliminate the threat to their political power. Many of the Tutsi Rwandans fled to refugee camps in bordering Uganda. They cried out to return to their homeland over the years, but the Rwandan government led by the Hutu majority blocked their peaceful return.

In the fall of 1990, the Rwandan Patriotic Front (RPF)—made up primarily of exiled Rwandans—invaded the country and began a three-year civil war. In August 1993, with assistance from the international community, a peace agreement was brokered that called for a democratically-elected government and the establishment of a broad-based transitional government. Unfortunately, that government was never installed. Instead, on April 6, 1994, following the death of the Rwandan president in a plane crash, a force of radical Hutus initiated their operation to exterminate the Tutsis and Hutus who supported the peace effort. The Hutus immediately claimed that the Tutsis shot down the plane, and the Hutu extremists began their reign of terror.

It was a bloody and dark time in the history of Rwanda, a country known as a beautiful agricultural gem with 1,000 green and lush hills that now flowed red with the blood of innocents. In addition to those killed, it is estimated that two million extremist Hutus fled to neighboring countries as refugees. For the most part, the world simply stood by and watched.

Grace was born in the capital city of Kigali, Rwanda in 1969. Her father was a landscaper at the French Embassy in Kigali, a good job that enabled his family of 14 to live a modest life. Grace's mom cared for the small home and their children. Theirs was not a Christian home even though, every Sunday, Grace's father sent her and her siblings out the door to follow a local pastor to his church. When they got home, there was no inquiry about what they learned at church; generally speaking, there was no encouragement of their faith from their parents. Grace did learn from her Sunday excursions that God was good and would be with her no matter what she experienced. She found this discovery to be a comfort and, from a young age, decided to believe in this loving God.

By the time Grace was in grade school, Hutu radio stations were broadcasting vicious hate propaganda against the Tutsis throughout the country. Grace was one of two Tutsis in her grade-school class of 60 students. She remembers regularly being called up to the front of the class only to be mocked by the Hutu students and the teacher. The only other Tutsi in her class chose to skip school and hide in the bushes to avoid the abuse.

When Grace's older sister passed the national exam, qualifying her to continue her secondary education, she went to pick up her certificate and discovered they had changed her score to a failing grade. It was to be expected. She was, after all, a Tutsi.

Grace's father told them of the civil war in 1959 which she and her siblings dubbed as "the old story." Little did they know that the hate and difficulties experienced then and since by the Tutsis would pale in comparison to the "new story" to come.

In 1990, the Rwandan Patriotic Front invaded Rwanda to obtain freedom for the Tutsi people, and many Tutsis living in Rwanda were rounded up and charged for conspiracy with the RPF. Grace's father was taken to a soccer stadium and starved and tortured along with the other Tutsis who were arrested. For over a week, they received no food and only an occasional drink of water. When the Hutus decided to let everyone return to their families, it was too late for most of them. Grace's father died on the way home.

Life became extremely difficult for Grace's family. Her father had been the sole breadwinner because women were not allowed to work outside the home. Grace's older brothers were not allowed to go to school, and they could not find employment. Because they had always lived in the city, Grace's family had no idea how to farm, but they had to learn in order to eat. What they were able to grow on a small patch of land behind their home became their means of survival. When the husband of one of Grace's sisters was killed, she had nowhere to go, so she and her four children moved back into the small house that was already bursting at the seams.

Grace was 25 years old and at home in bed the night of April 6, 1994 when she was awakened around 11:00 p.m. by a voice on the neighborhood loudspeaker proclaiming that the Tutsis had killed the president. People were instructed not to leave their homes. Roadblocks immediately went up to block fleeing Tutsis, for the killing was already underway throughout the country—and in Grace's neighborhood.

Grace's mother went to a Hutu neighbor with whom they had a good relationship and asked for protection. He defiantly said he had washed his hands of them because Tutsis had killed the president. He added, "God has given you over to be killed." That night, Grace's three brothers were killed with machetes and clubs. It took one brother two days to die. Grace and the rest of the family saw them murdered and heard their death screams.

Everyone ran for their lives. One sister, who had fled to the home of another neighbor with whose children she had often played, was murdered by her friends' father. Grace rushed to the home of a neighbor who had two wives, one a Hutu and the other a Tutsi. The Tutsi wife hid Grace under a bed. Her husband was a friend of Grace's father. Horrifically, he told Grace that, although he had helped to kill her brothers, he was not going to kill her. When the militia came to scour the neighborhood for any remaining Tutsis, Grace heard him say that he had killed a family of uncles but that seven had escaped, including one child. One of the militiamen responded, "We'll get him."

For two months, Grace hid under that bed and feared for her life every second of every day. The only time she emerged was to eat whatever meager portions she was provided. One day, the family unexpectedly fled, leaving her alone. Grace did not know it at the time, but the RPF army was retaking Kigali, and many Hutus began fleeing to neighboring countries. Grace took a chance and bolted to the nearby woods to hide. Many of her Tutsi neighbors were there as well but were under constant attack.

Grace spent six days in that forest without food. Her only source of water was an occasional mud puddle that formed when it rained and the moisture that gathered on the leaves in the morning. By the sixth day, she was drained of her will to survive. She later proclaimed, "I would have bought my own bullet if I could have done so."

At that point, the Hutus started burning the forest to force the Tutsis out into the open to be slaughtered. Grace staggered out and dropped to the ground. She was done, too emaciated to run or care. A Hutu militia member looked at her and decided not to waste his energy killing her. In her anguish, Grace thought, *He surely thinks I'm going to die on my own soon. Why should he help me by ending my misery?*

Another group of militia came upon Grace and, thinking she was dead, threw her into one of the mass grave pits. Yet, Grace continued to live as she laid for four days among what eventually became several hundred dead bodies, many of them tossed around and even on top of her. In her brief moments of consciousness, she recalled maggots crawling all over her.

On the fourth day, RPF troops secured the area. As they removed the bodies to bury them, the soldiers kicked each one that did not show signs of decomposition to make sure each person was dead. When a soldier stepped on Grace, she grunted. She was one of only two pulled from the mass grave who was still alive.

Grace survived, and slowly, her will to live returned; but she was done with God. She began to believe that what she had believed in church as a young girl was a lie. God had not been there when she, her family, her friends, and her country needed Him. He had allowed hundreds of thousands to be brutally murdered, raped, and injured. Grace had encountered the face of evil. How could she believe in a God who allowed what seemed worse than Hell to occur in her homeland and to those she loved?

The widows with whom she now regularly sewed—Maleb, Theresa, and Jeanne—cried with Grace, held her hand, and shared their own stories of the genocide and their hope in Jesus Christ.

Theresa and Maleb knew each other before everyone scattered during the genocide. Life had been hard, particularly for Theresa and her six children. When the two women reunited in the marketplace, their hope was to put at least one meal on the table for their families from each day's sales. They came up with an idea to put their products together and look for other sewing women who could add variety to the items they offered to buyers.

Theresa brought in Jeanne, who had been in a Congolese refugee camp prior to the genocide. In addition to losing her husband, she had lost three sons in the camp and was so sick she went into a coma. She remained in the coma for so long that her limbs were drawn to her core in a fetal position, and her weight dropped to a mere 60 pounds. Eventually, Jeanne came out of her coma, and the Red Cross worked to rehabilitate her. She returned to Rwanda following the genocide and continued to regain her health while taking care of her three children and her mother. Jeanne became a street vendor, illegally selling avocados and oranges wherever she could to feed her family.

Especially given her difficult circumstances, she was excited to join the sewing group. She didn't have a lot of fabric and only had a few products to sell, but she knew the basics of sewing, and the other ladies helped her with supplies, ideas, and in improving her skills.

A Healing Faith

Grace struggled to understand their faith in a God who she was convinced had abandoned her, yet she wanted her sewing friends to understand, so she continued her story. They listened intently, understanding her agony.

Over the next five years after her deliverance from the mass grave, Grace married the soldier who pulled her from the pile of dead bodies. She went to work in an orphanage and began to think there might be some hope for her and the future of her family. She was pregnant with their fourth child when the news came that her soldier husband had been killed in a battle with exiled Hutu extremists along the Congo border. Grace was so traumatized that she slipped into a coma, and she wasn't even aware when she gave birth to their daughter. To make matters worse, when Grace regained consciousness, she was informed that she had lost her job. She had nowhere to go but to her mother-in-law's home, a tiny, grass-thatched house. Grace couldn't feed her four children and, once again, was drained of all hope. Her one surviving brother started selling car tires in the marketplace and invited Grace to work for him. They got by until the market caught fire and they lost everything. Grace then isolated herself in her mother-in-law's home, and her despair was so great it was feared she'd take her own life, leading her sister-in-law to bring her to the sewing ladies.

The women continued to pray together, share their joys and sorrows, and sing hymns every day while they sewed. They invited pastors and others who were knowledgeable about the scriptures to talk about faith and study about God with them. Grace slowly began to seek out the Bible verses that she learned before the genocide, especially those that offered comfort and encouragement. She kept reading and listening. Often, Grace tried to give her heart to God, but her thoughts invariably returned to the hatred, bitterness, and anger that haunted her. *Why should I pray? What is the point? I can't forgive.* The Hutus had tried to kill her physically, and now, Satan was striving to steal her heart and soul.

In the years that followed, Grace continued sewing with the ladies, and the group added members while making enough money to meet their needs.

Theresa brought Vestine to the group in 2002, and Jeanne did the same with her addition of Beata. Their stories were similarly haunting. Vestine's mother died in the genocide, and her father remarried and rejected his daughter. She had no shoes or clothes other than what she wore, and she rarely ate. She said she was dejected, alone, and "completely worn out." She didn't know how to sew and couldn't afford to buy any material. The ladies immediately embraced her as part of the group and began teaching her how to sew. They gave her their material so she could get started selling simple items and become self-sustaining. Vestine was no longer alone. She experienced unconditional love like never before.

Beata was four months pregnant when she was forced to move back into her family's home after her husband abandoned her. Her parents were impoverished, so Beata started vending vegetables on the streets to feed them and her siblings. All 13 of them were living together in a one-bedroom house. On a good day, Beata's vending provided one meal of potatoes and beans. After Beata joined the group, the ladies paid her more than their established rate for the products she completed in order to encourage her. Beata gratefully recalls that, with her first paycheck of $15, she celebrated by buying beef and rice for her family— the first time they had eaten either item in seven years. She was even able to purchase some bananas for her child.

These six resourceful yet inexperienced businesswomen rented a veranda and continued to sew and sell together. In 2004, they formed *Koperative Amahoro ava hejuru* as an association. "Amahoro ava hejuru" translates to "peace comes from above." Like *shalom* in Hebrew, *amahoro* has a much wider meaning than the normal translation. It encompasses everything to do with internal and external peace, connection, and wholeness. With all they had endured as a result of the genocide, each woman within this special group found her personal peace with God. Some of the women were Tutsi survivors who had lost their husbands; others were Hutus whose husbands had done the killing and had been lost in the fighting or to prison. But their pasts no longer weighed them down. They had found peace with each other, and their hearts had been healed.

Grace had also been healed. One year earlier, she had heard a pastor's sermon that confronted her inability to forgive. "If you haven't forgiven, you haven't been forgiven," her pastor stated forthrightly. "So why are you here?" Grace's heart and mind were moved in a way she had never experienced. She forgave those who had traumatized or murdered her family and friends. She asked God to forgive her for once proclaiming that there was no God, and she immediately experienced personal peace she had never before thought was available. Grace, the amazing survivor, immediately knew she had just experienced God's amazing grace.

They Needed a Leader

Koperative Amahoro ava hejuru became an informal yet deeply binding association. The women were committed to one another and to their business, but they had no internal rules and no consistent marketing plan for their products. Their gift was to sew and heal hearts together, but they wanted to grow the business further and continue to advance their families out of poverty. What they needed was a leader.

While she wasn't selected or nominated to do so, Grace was compelled to see what she could do to help develop the organization. She knew very little about what makes a business work, so she inquired of other successful business owners and learned from them. The Rwandan government created the Rwanda Development Board to help train and promote small business, and Grace sought their input and resources. The sewing group had a wonderful story and top-quality, hand-sewn products. Their biggest challenge was getting access to consistent customers. Grace created cards and brochures that told the story of the ladies and their products and began placing them around the city. She convinced *Hôtel des Mille Collines* (aka Hotel Rwanda) to allow them to establish a booth to sell their products at the hotel. Through consistent and focused marketing, their sales started increasing. As their exposure grew, so did their reputation for high-quality, creative products.

Grace methodically marketed the group and their products, and she became the manager and leader they needed. Today, she remains the economic engine of *Koperative Amahoro ava hejuru*. Grace attributes her success in helping grow the business to finally giving her heart and mind to God.

The business model remains simple. The group establishes what items are to be created, the price to be paid to the person who is sewing for each completed product, and the price at which each will be sold. Each woman determines what she wants to sew and how many hours she wants to work. They often work together using an assembly-line approach and equally share the income for the finished products. They are paid at the end of each month for the products produced plus their equal share of the profits for the products sold. Grace is paid an extra $65 each month to manage and market the business.

As the business grew, so did the number of hearts that were healed. Grace brought Florence into the group, as did Jeanne with Rose Mary and Beata with Pascaline.

Florence was a widow with no home for her three children, no means of feeding her family, and no experience sewing.

Rose Mary was orphaned before the genocide when her father died of a heart attack. She had to drop out of school to help her mother care for her five siblings by selling groceries on the streets. The women taught Rose Mary how to sew by drawing lines on paper so she could practice stitching. Rose Mary had a difficult time learning, but the ladies were patient and gladly followed through on Rose Mary's request that they pray for her to become good at sewing.

Pascaline was the oldest of five siblings whose family was extremely poor, living in a collapsing mud and thatched house with no concrete, no doors, no water, no electricity, and nothing to eat. They were lucky to eat one meal a day that consisted of potatoes and beans. She used her first paycheck to buy food for her family previously beyond their imagination: beef, chicken, and rice.

This impressive group of humble women grew the business to the level that, in 2009, *Koperative Amahoro ava hejuru* was formally granted registration as a cooperative by the Rwandan government. How did they celebrate? By praising God together joyfully with prayer, singing, and dancing. Grace's marketing efforts, in combination with the high quality of the colorful products offered, have paid off. They now participate in local and international trade shows and have cultivated word-of-mouth awareness at places like the U.S. Embassy in Kigali. Their products are now distributed in the United States through the

School of Business and Entrepreneurship program at Cuyahoga Valley Christian Academy (www.shyadesigns.com). The products have become so popular that *Koperative Amahoro ava hejuru* now outsources much of its sewing to other women in small shops. Overall, the co-op supports 74 families, including those of the nine co-op members.

The "Amahoro sewing ladies," as they are affectionately known, along with the help of many friends made along the way, have consistently grown the cooperative's revenue and profit. Their product selection has expanded to feature 70 different African-themed items created from brilliant Rwandan fabric. The items include laptop, shopping, and duffel bags; African animal-themed wall hangings; iPad covers; kitchen aprons; children's animal-themed backpacks; Christmas stockings; and many other useful products.

In 2017, *Koperative Amahoro ava hejuru* earned approximately $17,000 in revenue with net profit of about $6,000 on which they will pay 14 percent in tax. On this amount, each of the women make between $100-$150 per month for the items they sew plus their equal share of the profit.

Compared to what is earned in developed countries, these amounts may seem insignificant. But in Rwanda, and for these previously hopeless ladies, it is a true success story, one that has economically and emotionally changed the trajectory of the women's lives and the lives of their descendants for generations to come. In Rwanda, individuals share the cost of their children's education, and getting children educated in the better schools can be expensive. For example, it cost Pascaline about $500 a year to send her daughter to high school, which is approximately 33 percent of her annual income, not including cooperative profit distributions. Still, without any direct help from the outside, these women have worked their families out of poverty, provided for their children's education, and given their families hope for their future. Grace said,

I have four children—two sons and two daughters. I never remarried but have been able to provide my children with a good education. My oldest son has graduated from college and is working. I have raised my children to, likewise, put themselves in a position to someday take care of their children, my grandchildren. I also own my home and some smaller rental houses behind my home. I have a savings account to make sure we don't again become impoverished.

The greatest blessing is that my children know Christ; we pray and share our faith together.

Pascaline recognizes her blessings with gratefulness. She said,

Beata knew my situation and brought me here. I put myself in the hands of these women, and they taught me how to sew. In the morning, we have prayers and sharing. When I face challenges, my friends here pray with me. Because of them and their prayers, I have grown spiritually.

Thanks to Amahoro, we are not poor anymore. I have been able to send my daughter to school. I have also built a new home for my family and take care of them. Amahoro means "peace", and as the name says, I received peace in my heart here.

Theresa said she came to the sewing group with nothing.

I was a widow with six children. My children have all graduated and are married with their own children. I have 11 grandchildren. I own my home, and although I am a widow, I am never lonely because of the Amahoro women around me. I love that we pray together every morning and thank God for his provisions and what He will do in the future.

Maleb said she gains knowledge from the other women.

> If I have a problem, they all pray with me. My physical and spiritual needs have been met through Amahoro. This is my first family, and I am now married with my own family. I love that we have been able to impact others for God's glory through this business.

Jeanne's three children are educated, one having completed university courses. She said,

> I am able to feed and care for everyone in my family, and I own my home. Everything good that I have is because of Amahoro. We do not put money first in our business. Healing hearts is first. For new members, we help them find a way to solve problems. Housing is the biggest problem, and we help with a place to stay until they can purchase their own home. If I can stretch, I can dance and have joy. I love to lead the group in dancing while we praise the Lord.

Vestine knows her heart has been healed through God's love displayed through her friends in the group. She said,

> Everyone prayed for me when I told them my story, and I felt their love. We are women who work together and solve problems together. We love each other. We are a family.

Beata affirms the depth of their relationships with each other.

> The women here are like family with whom to share challenges. Problems don't stick with me because I am able to share them with my friends, and they pray for me.

Beata is able to care for her mother who lives with her, and her daughter has graduated from high school. Two years after joining the group, she was able to expand her family's home by adding two rooms and paying off the loan on the home. "Grace helped me," Beata said. "God bless Grace for that."

Florence has also been able to send her children to school, buy a home, and provide food for everyone in her family. She noted,

> All of the women here go to different churches, but we share one Bible. There is no difference of religion for us. We don't recognize tribes. We all look to Christ as our Savior.

Rose Mary was married in 2015. Regarding her wedding, she said, "Because I considered all of the women of Amahoro to also be my mothers, they gave me away." She continued,

> I love sewing because it is a safe haven for me. I was in extreme poverty but have now learned a skill and am able to care for my family. I have also grown spiritually with the women through their prayers.

Community Impact

Once viewed with pity, the Amahoro sewing ladies are now respected in their communities and recognized for their achievements. They are much more grateful to God than they are proud of anything they have done. They consider their accomplishments to be blessings from God, and they see their business and profession as a calling. It is their ministry, one that enables them to help lift others as they have been lifted.

Keys to Their Success

The ladies have used their profits wisely. As a cooperative, they have invested in loans to members to purchase their homes and in the acquisition of the building that houses their common sewing area and their pedal-powered sewing machines. It also contains a retail outlet that has become a popular destination for locals and visitors to Kigali. Their building, owned by the cooperative, is today worth $79,000.

The keys to their success are like their business—simple yet significantly impactful. They've done their best to learn, understand, and practice biblical principles in their relationships and in their business. They work hard and focus on producing quality products that meet the needs of their customers, and they don't fear taking thoughtful, calculated risks. They do what they say they will do when they say they will do it by meeting deadlines and offering top-notch customer service. They refuse to compromise their integrity and honesty. It is essential to them to glorify God in how they run a profitable business, and they understand that they honor God by having pure motives.

National Healing

Thanks to thoughtful and inspirational post-genocide leadership in the Rwandan government, the country and its citizens have made tremendous progress toward healing the deep and devastating wounds of the 1994 genocide. The government adopted a Christ-centered plan to foster forgiveness, reconciliation, and hope for the future. No tribes are officially recognized; they are all Rwandan. The government has taken a zero-tolerance stance against corruption, resulting in Rwandans having a safe country where they can work to better themselves and their families. Grace said,

> We have good leadership today—gender equality, no segregation, very little crime. Now, women can go to the bank, take loans, and do business just like the men. As long as God keeps giving us good leadership, I have hope for our developing country and for a better life for my family.

Understandably, the fears of the past have not been fully overcome. Grace's greatest concern, as with most Rwandans of her generation, is, *What if this happens again?* "I still have nightmares of the militia chasing me," Grace said, adding that she shares her fears with her friends at the cooperative, and they pray together aloud. She continued,

> Nothing else can heal us. We all have experienced trauma and even torture. Only our shared prayers give us peace. I understand that my trust can only be in God—not in man. It is hard to realize that your neighbor can turn on you and kill your family. God gave man free will, and sometimes, Satan gets hold of humans, and they make bad and even evil choices.
>
> It hasn't been easy, but together, through the grace of God, we have found a way not to let our past encumber us nor undermine our hope for the future. My hope is solely in Jesus. The promises of Jesus give me the greatest hope!

It is clear that the ladies of *Koperative Amahoro ava hejuru* stitch with a purpose—sowing peace with their sewing. For Grace, it is a way to bring the Lord glory.

> God brought me here to be a living testimony … to share my story with other people so they can say, "Wow! God really can do amazing things with your life no matter what you came from." God didn't bring me into the world to be a decoration like a flower. My life has been difficult at times, but God has allowed and empowered me to share my story with other women who struggle the way I struggled previously. God helped me to survive for the purpose of helping other women. I share what I have with others; I share the opportunity that was shared with me. I once felt valueless and wished God had left me to die in the pile of bodies. Once I realized that God saved me for a purpose and that He values and loves me no matter what, it became easy for me to love and value others regardless of their situation.

Forgiveness is a thread that binds the tapestry of Grace's life and purpose. What does that forgiveness look like? It is the widow of the man who killed her uncle's family coming to visit Grace with her daughter in tow. She came to ask for Grace's forgiveness. Grace not only granted it but taught the widow's daughter how to sew so she could help support the family because they couldn't afford to send her to school.

Forgiveness is Grace taking the wife of a man in prison to see him for a visit, the same man who had helped kill her family. When he saw Grace and asked why she had come, she responded, "I've come to forgive you. I don't believe it was you but Satan who overtook you. I forgive you for what you did to my family." Grace continues to help his family by providing food.

Grace has also helped to heal the guilt-shackled and shame-ridden hearts of the families of the perpetrators of the genocide by showing them her healed heart and offering to them the forgiveness and peace that she so treasures.

It is important to note that Grace's acts of forgiveness and reconciliation are not uncommon in Rwanda. Similar acts have taken place by the thousands—perhaps, hundreds of thousands—throughout the country. The government has placed Rwanda's hope for the future in Christ's teachings, and it has worked diligently to provide the platforms, education, and encouragement for the people of their nation to forgive, reconcile, and advance cohesively into the future.

Rwandans hope never to forget where the evil of genocide took them so they can remain united in their hope. They take pride in the way they are overcoming the atrocities they have endured. Grace and the Amahoro sewing ladies want people to know that, despite the problems and challenges the people of their country have experienced, Rwandans are good, hopeful, loving, and hard-working people who went through genocide and have chosen to be forgivers and reconcilers—not victims. They are people who have hope through Jesus Christ.

Looking Toward the Future

It is against this backdrop that, like any business owner, Grace and the cooperative members constantly think about how best to continue to grow the business into the future. In order to help facilitate the growth of the Amahoro Cooperative and to also help other women become self-reliant, Grace has opened an additional business and retail outlet, Komera Creation, that combines handmade crafts created by local women along with the items sewn by the Amahoro ladies. (Komera in the Kinyarwandan language means "courage" or "be strong.") There are also plans to open a trade school and teach the poorest of the poor how to sew so they, too, can enjoy the immense satisfaction of working their way out of poverty.

Grace hopes to hire and train a business development manager and perhaps even a business manager so *Koperative Amahoro ava hejuru* can continue to grow when she retires.

It is also imperative for the women that they continue to bring into the cooperative the next generation of sewing ladies. They are all committed to ensuring that the growth and success of the business continues beyond their years.

After all, there are many hearts out there that need healing.

Personal Reflection and Group Discussion

1. In relative terms, the business size and revenue of the Amahoro sewing ladies is miniscule, but the impact the sewing ladies have made on the lives they touch is immense. What understanding about how God works do you derive from this contrast?

2. For the Amahoro sewing ladies, healing hearts is more important than money. What is more important than money for you? Does your allocation of time and resources reflect this? If not, what will you do to change that?

3. In what ways can you display more love and care for those with whom you work?

4. What is the most significant thing for which you've had to forgive others? What was the outcome of your willingness to forgive for you and for them?

5. Grace said, "God helped me to survive for the purpose of helping other women. I share what I have with others." How does this statement and her actions inspire you to greater service for God?

6. What other spiritual, business, and personal concepts and practices noted in this chapter stood out to you? How will you integrate them into your life and/or business?

6

CLEARING THE PATH:
GLOBAL PALM RESOURCES
HOLDINGS LIMITED

Pontianak, Indonesia

BLEND INCESSANT CURIOSITY, an insatiable thirst for learning, and an infectiously warm, caring, and jovial nature, and you have a trusted leader of character, Dr. Suparno Adijanto, who clears the path for others to grow and thrive.

He didn't become a path clearer overnight, though. First, Suparno's path had to be cleared by others, and when he encountered crossroads, he had to make life-changing choices about which direction to take. Today, Suparno recognizes and is grateful for those who helped to clear his path and keep him on, as he likes to call it, "the exciting path."

It started with Tan Lim Hian, also known as "Adijanto", Suparno's father and his first path-clearer. Adijanto's father grew up in a wealthy family in China and didn't have to work, so he learned martial arts and became a trusted leader of the 500 troops who protected the village in which they lived. When his troops were ambushed and defeated, Adijanto's father migrated to Pontianak, Indonesia where he met his wife and eventually had eight children with her.

Indonesia is an archipelago comprised of thousands of islands in Southeast Asia. Pontianak was founded as a trading station located on the island of Borneo and built on the delta of the Kapuas River, the longest river in Indonesia. Pontianak is located precisely on the equator and is the capital of the Indonesian province of West Kalimantan, a historically important trading port.

It was there that Adijanto became an entrepreneur.

He started early, going to work at age 12 to help support his parents and siblings because his father had no knowledge of work or business due to his entitled childhood. Despite only studying until grade six, Adijanto started buying, selling, and trading inexpensive goods in and around Pontianak from a small boat on the Kapuas. Later, he went to work in the coffee business for a gentleman who was impressed by Adijanto's strong work ethic, honesty, and integrity. They eventually became partners, and Adijanto helped to expand the business.

Adijanto left the partnership in 1952 to begin his own trading company. After the Vietnam War started three years later, rubber became in great demand and prompted the industrious Adijanto to launch a rubber company around the same time that he married Ang Tje Kiang and started a family. As the war wound down and demand for rubber decreased, Adijanto started a timber business headquartered in Pontianak. Each of his five sons joined Adijanto in the business, beginning with the oldest in 1978. It eventually became one of the largest timber companies in the country.

Over time, Adijanto and his sons vertically integrated by sending the timber they logged to sawmills they owned. Always the innovator, Adijanto figured out how to use timber and its waste to become one of the world's largest tropical plywood and chipboard manufacturers. He even launched a company to produce the adhesive needed to make the plywood and chipboard. They expanded further and began manufacturing linoleum and wood laminates for bowling alleys, flooring, and outdoor use. By the mid-1990s, Adijanto's timber business was completely vertically integrated with every supply chain for the timber company under their ownership. They were involved in everything from harvesting the lumber to using it and its by-products to manufacture a wide variety of wood and paper products.

Finding Joy

Suparno, the youngest of Adijanto's five boys, joined the business in 1982, but his path had been cleared and direction established many years earlier. When Suparno was six years old, the Chinese schools in Indonesia were closed due to political upheaval. Although Adijanto had little education, he highly valued learning and wanted his children to receive the best education possible. So he established a second home in Singapore and moved his family there. Suparno and his four brothers and two sisters continued their schooling while Adijanto commuted between Singapore and Jakarta to oversee his businesses.

Later, Suparno was sent to London to live with his other siblings and attend high school. When he was 17, his sister took him to an international church and introduced Suparno to a community of Christian students of varying nationalities. His parents weren't Christian, so Suparno knew very little about the faith. What he did have was a lot of unanswered questions about why people couldn't get along with one another and ended up in wars like the one in Vietnam. He observed and was fascinated by how these students from totally different cultures and backgrounds found unity in Christ. Theirs was a loving community inspired by their common belief in Jesus and His teachings.

The new friends took an interest in Suparno, and after church, they went to lunch together and talked about what they were learning. They shared with Suparno their love of the Bible and mentored him in the faith. He was encouraged to study the Bible and meditate on God's Word so he could call on it when needed. "To this day," Suparno declared, "one of my greatest joys is studying God's Word and discovering biblical truths and then helping others understand them."

Before long, Suparno realized that his education and other future pursuits could not bring him happiness unless he had a bigger purpose—God's purpose. He repented of his sins and gave his life to Jesus Christ. He said,

> I learned that life is not a dot—but an eternal line. Not 70 to 80 years here on Earth—but eternity. Second Corinthians 4:18 became my life verse. "So we fix our eyes not on what is seen, but on what is unseen, since what is seen is temporary, but what is unseen is eternal." At the end of my life, God will call on me to account for that which He entrusted to me. This Bible verse encourages us to focus on what is unseen. I understand that certain things like the souls of men and obedience to God will last for eternity. On the other hand, worldly things like money, materials, power, and fame are temporary. This realization leads me to constantly ask, "What would you have me do, Lord?"

From that day forward, Suparno continued to read and study the Bible daily and then prayerfully meditate on what that day's particular Scripture passage meant for his life. "When I prayerfully meditate on God's Word," Suparno said, "He takes my understanding to a higher level." He determined not to lose his soul to gain the world (Matthew 16:26).

Suparno completed his Bachelor of Economics degree with honors at University College in London and his Master of Business Administration degree at the University of Bradford in England. He returned to Indonesia at the age of 22 and joined the family business. His astute father perceived something different about Suparno. Although he was thoroughly disciplined, Adijanto noticed that his son didn't do well when forced into highly structured situations. Adijanto had always wanted one of his sons to have a doctorate in order to gain additional perspective and felt Suparno should be given the opportunity. In 1984, Suparno enrolled at Georgia State University in Atlanta, Georgia, and it was there that he met the next path clearer in his life—his future wife, See Mun Leong.

See Mun

The daughter of Chinese and Buddhist parents, See Mun grew up in Ipoh, Malaysia. They were hard workers; her mother owned and ran a retail store, and her father worked in mining and owned a restaurant. Both were determined to help set the trajectory of See Mun's future with a good education. She was sent to a Methodist mission school at the age of six to begin her education and learn English. Her parents believed that a Christian school would give her a strong moral foundation and quality education. An unexpected turn of events came when See Mun was in high school and an old high school friend of See Mun's mother returned to Malaysia from the United States, reconnecting with the family after being apart for 30 years. He convinced See Mun's mother and father that a degree from a college in the United States could be invaluable for See Mun's future. He helped to find a host family for her in Atlanta, and shortly thereafter, she enrolled at Georgia State University.

See Mun and Suparno first saw each other in the classroom where he was a graduate assistant. Later, they were formally introduced to one another by a mutual friend and were immediately attracted to each other. With a twinkle in her eyes, See Mun shared how Suparno stretched their first date out over three days. On the Wednesday of their date, Suparno asked See Mun to help him find a gift for a mutual friend who was graduating that coming Saturday. They shopped for several hours on Wednesday and then again on Thursday, but Suparno wasn't satisfied with anything they found. It wasn't until Friday night, right before the mall closed, that they found the gift. "Well, I did have to find the *perfect* gift," Suparno explained with a playful grin.

They continued to date while Suparno achieved his doctorate and See Mun completed her undergraduate work. She worked for a year and then went back to school to attain a master's degree in business management. See Mun says she was most impressed with Suparno's character. He didn't party like most of the students. He studied, went to church, and looked out for the family business. Most importantly, she was attracted to his compassionate heart as he helped Vietnamese refugees and their children in his spare time, including teaching a Sunday school class for the Vietnamese children.

See Mun was introduced to Christianity through her Methodist mission school and the Methodist church she later attended, but her spiritual growth had been gradual. When she joined a small Indonesian Christian fellowship in Atlanta, her faith accelerated. She was baptized and started to learn from her Christian friends how to turn the knowledge she was receiving from her disciplined Bible study into practical application for her life. Plus, See Mun found in Suparno someone with whom she could have intimate conversations about their faith—and their hopes and dreams for the future. They married in 1988 and lived in California where Suparno gained international work experience as the president of Westpont International Trading Company, a U.S.-based trading company that deals in commodity trading between Southeast Asia and the United States. One year later, they returned to Indonesia, and the first of their three children, Jonathan, was born in 1990, followed by Carina and Justin.

Understanding His Unique Abilities

Suparno's responsibilities in the family businesses were different than those of his siblings. Adijanto recognized that his son needed freedom to create in order to be energized and that Suparno seemed to thrive in unsettled situations that needed to be improved. With his four brothers running various companies, Suparno was given the freedom to diversify the businesses, guide the investment of the profits, improve efficiency, and increase value through integrating technology and developing an overall strategic plan to grow and thrive. "This was the perfect role for me," Suparno said. "My father cleared the way, and I felt the Lord's hand guide me onto the path."

Living His Faith at Work

At the same time when Suparno was busy reinventing the family business, he also began contemplating how he could better live out his faith in his work. He observed that, even though there were more Christian business owners than ever in his predominantly Muslim country, they continued to separate their faith from their business. As a result, many were still corrupt in their business practices. Suparno understood that he should live as a believer in Jesus Christ seven days a week and in everything he did. He was convinced that God had called him to the family business and had created him for exactly what he was doing. It dawned on him that he was in ministry, melding together his professional and spiritual life as one.

Indonesia was and remains a difficult place for Christians to live out their beliefs in their businesses. It is the world's fourth most populated country and the most populous Muslim-majority country. According to Suparno, people of Protestant and Catholic faiths, while increasing, still account for less than 10 percent of the total population.

In addition, a large percentage of Indonesia's residents are impoverished—Suparno estimates this number is over 20 percent—and are therefore focused on survival.

Another influence is Indonesians of Chinese descent, some of which are Christian but who control a significant portion of the privately-owned commerce and wealth in the country.

Then, there is corruption. Transparency International, in its inaugural 1995 Corruption Perceptions Index, ranked Indonesia the most corrupt nation of 41 countries rated worldwide. Even in 2016, according to the latest data available, it remained 88th of 168 countries listed. Despite others' belief systems and the corruption, Suparno committed to help run the family business with integrity and in accordance with biblical principles. He'd later learn that doing so would require every ounce of faith he could muster.

"It is an interesting phenomenon," said Suparno, "that while the path before us continues to be cleared, we are often concurrently clearing the path for others." In 1991, he proposed to his family that, in addition to diversifying their business holdings, they should take some of their larger businesses public and open the door for non-family investors. To do so in Indonesia doesn't necessarily dilute the family holdings to a minority. On the contrary, to this day, the family holds approximately 70 percent of the shares of all their publicly traded companies.

Even though the family continues to control the shares and the vote, being a publicly traded company requires complete transparency, robust reporting, accountability, auditing, and well-defined, independent corporate governance. Suparno believed this strategy was going to facilitate the family companies being operated professionally and ethically into the future. Additionally, the companies were entering their third generation, and many of the family members that someday were to become shareholders were not going to work in the family business. There are now 24 third-generation family members that live all over the world, and Suparno laughingly comments that many "are too educated to be in commodities." He desired for them to have a choice of whether to work in one of the family businesses. In addition, he wanted to create a market for their shares if, at any time, they opted to sell and invest elsewhere.

One of the companies taken public in 1991 was Kurnia Kapuas Glue Industries, later renamed as Resource Alam Indonesia, which is listed in Jakarta. (*Alam* translates to "natural.") This was the adhesive company originally founded in 1981 to support the timber byproduct business that grew to have an international reach. Also taken public in 1995 was Harrison Holdings Limited, Malaysia's oldest, largest, and most-established sales, marketing, and warehousing company. The distribution division of the company is involved in distributing fast-moving consumer products for major multinational companies like Nestle, Malex, and Asia Pacific Brewery as well as building materials, engineering products, fine wines, and agricultural and industrial chemicals. Harrison's assets also include a shipping and logistics operation and a travel agency.

A new private commodity company later known as Global Palm Resources was added to the family's businesses in 1991. Global Palm cultivates, harvests, and processes palm oil fruit into crude palm oil that is sold to be further refined for use in cosmetics and food products. The diversification continued with a 1994 investment in Energy Equity Corporation, an Australian public energy company based in Perth, Australia. Suparno's family bought into the company at around 35 cents per share and became Energy Equity's largest shareholder. Suparno helped Energy Equity negotiate with the Indonesian government its independent power-purchase agreement. This resulted in Energy Equity building the first independent gas-fired power plant to sell to the Indonesian grid. Their stock price increased to $2.00 over the next three years, and the company's capitalization almost reached $1 billion in Australian dollars.

Within a decade, Suparno and his siblings had risen to the challenge and helped expand the family's holdings beyond the timber business into China, Hong Kong, Singapore, Indonesia, Malaysia, Australia, and Thailand. By 1996, the family owned 80 companies and had over 20,000 employees. However, Suparno was troubled that there was no synergy among the companies. At the same time, he was led by God to read Bob Buford's life-altering book, *Halftime*. Suparno realized that he needed to shift from pursuing success to significance. He prayed, seeking clarity and direction regarding God's purposes for him, and the Lord placed Isaiah 57:14 on his heart:

> And it will be said: "Build up, build up, prepare the road! Remove the obstacles out of the way of my people."

He took this to mean that he needed to live more significantly, but he was not yet sure about what direction to take. It was a couple of years later that Suparno realized that the verse was a calling for him to help build up and prepare the path and remove the obstacles not just for his family's business but also for foreign ministries to set up operations in Indonesia.

Then, a flood of events outside of their control presented unexpected dilemmas for the businesses—and forced Suparno and his family to make some very difficult decisions.

Difficult Decisions

The 1997-98 financial crisis in Asia nearly destroyed the economies of Indonesia, South Korea, and Thailand. It started in Thailand and was driven by risky financial overextension led by massive real estate development. Other countries' economies—Hong Kong, Korea, Malaysia, and the Philippines—were severely affected as well. Brunei, China, Singapore, Taiwan, and Vietnam also suffered but were less impacted.

In Indonesia, the exchange rate on their currency, the rupiah, went from 2,400 per $1.00 to as high as 17,000 per $1.00 before settling at around 12,000 per $1.00. Interest rates for borrowing the rupiah went as high as 100 percent. The Indonesian government and the businesses there that had borrowed U.S. dollars were devastated. Seven of the 10 largest banks collapsed, and it took government intervention to save the remaining three banks. Sporadic rioting followed sharp price increases caused by a drastic devaluation of the rupiah. The central government lost control, and there was widespread lawlessness and extortion. The remaining banks and government confiscated enormous amounts of assets from borrowers. A significant number of families who owned businesses lost everything, and Suparno's family and their businesses were under tremendous stress.

It was a frightening time for Suparno and his family. In May 1998, when many in Indonesia demonstrated against the president, five student protesters were gunned downed by government troops, igniting riots across the country. Thousands of businesses and homes were looted and burned. Over 1,000 people died, and the military was in chaos. Suparno's family members were permanent residents in Singapore, and the Singapore government sent several Singapore Airlines jumbo jets to extract their citizens living in Indonesia. Suparno, his family, and some friends decided to drive in a convoy to the airport even though it was dangerous to do so. They made it to the airport but were met by thousands of others who were also trying to get out. The family prayed fervently and were finally able to acquire a flight to Singapore. Two weeks later, the Indonesian president was removed from office, and a new president was appointed with a promise of elections within a year. Throughout that chaotic time, Suparno and his family were encouraged and found hope as they read their Bibles and shared Bible verses. Psalm 91:7 was particularly meaningful to them: "A thousand may fall at your side, ten thousand at your right hand, but it will not come near you."

Suparno's family's businesses were able to survive because they had fairly low debt, exported a significant amount of the products they produced, were diversified into other countries and businesses, and were able to strategically divest of some of their holdings. However, during and following the financial crisis, the Indonesian government made two decisions that brought Suparno and his family to a crossroads. They had to either dramatically change their core business holdings and approach to diversification or watch their primary businesses die a slow death.

The first decision had to be made when the government refused to pay Energy Equity Corporation the foreign-exchange-adjusted contract prices for electricity. This forced Energy Equity to sell at a rate based on the rupiah at 2,400 when the prevailing exchange was 12,000. The company's per-share price went from $2.00 to one cent. It was on the brink of insolvency, and the family's investment was all but lost.

The second decision after the crisis came in 1999 when the government started reducing on an annual basis the amount of timber that could be harvested by setting decreasing quotas. Suparno's family had to buy timber from other companies but continued to lose money. Lawlessness set in throughout the industry as corrupt operators did whatever they could, legal or not, to remain in business. Suparno and his family were not willing to compromise their values rooted in fairness and honesty. By the early 2000s, it became clear to the family that they were going to be forced out of the timber business.

To complicate matters further, the family owned a bank, and during the crisis, customers could not make their loan payments. The family had to close the bank. The government insured the bank's deposits, protecting the customers, but the government sought to recoup what they had paid to the depositors from Suparno's family. The government tried to force the family to sell any remaining assets that had value and reimburse them. Many government officials were extorting others in similar situations and threatening them with arrest. Suparno was selected to represent his family in the negotiations with the government.

Even though it accounted for 70 percent of the family's business revenue, a prayerful decision was made in 2001 to begin methodically shutting down the timber business and all other timber-related operations in Indonesia by 2005. Unfortunately, 15,000 workers were laid off in the process. This resulted in the family incurring severance payouts in excess of $10 million. The family was determined to provide for their workers instead of claiming insolvency even though doing so would necessitate liquidating other valuable assets to make the payments. Suparno had been to Pontianak to review the financials for all the family's holdings and was convinced that they'd soon be unable to meet their monthly obligations. The combination of issues could eventually force them into liquidation.

This was a low point for Suparno, and his trust in God was being severely tested. On the flight home to Jakarta, Suparno opted against his preferred aisle seat and chose a window seat instead. It was late in the day, and the sun was low on the horizon. As he peered out the window, he was suddenly struck by the beauty of the deep blue sky contrasted against the vibrant colors dancing off the clouds on the horizon. He marveled at the incredible magnitude of God's creation and the immeasurable power of the Creator. At that moment, Suparno felt the Lord's wonderful peace and sensed an inner voice reassuring him that God was much bigger than the problems faced by his family and that the God who created everything could certainly carry them through anything. So instead of succumbing to his own, limited understanding and reacting accordingly, Suparno summoned his faith, determined not to waver from seeking and following God's will. He chose to follow God's path to help his family work through the many complicated and seemingly overwhelming issues. It became an intense day-by-day, minute-by-minute test, but eventually, Suparno's prayers for direction began being answered. God provided for his faithful servant and his family in miraculous proportions.

Resolution

Suparno was led by the Lord to seek advice wisely from those he respected. A friend at the World Bank advised him not to go heavily into debt or sell viable assets to repay the government for the bank deposit insurance payments. He reminded Suparno that the family had owned and managed the bank with integrity and had done nothing wrong and were not responsible for the economic crisis that caused the bank to fail. Besides, he advised, the family had already lost their entire investment, and the deposit insurance provided by the government was designed for this exact type of situation to avert chaos in the country. Suparno began his negotiations and surprisingly discovered that the government officials with whom he was meeting were God-fearing individuals and not involved in any extortion. The government negotiated in good faith and allowed the family to redeem the government bonds they owned at face value to cover the government's insurance payouts. Although the family felt they were not obligated to repay the government anything, they were ecstatic with this win-win solution.

Concurrently, a California energy company under the same contract as Energy Equity sued the Indonesian government and won a $300 million judgment. Suparno believed that suing the government would harm Energy Equity and his family's other business holdings in the long run and decided not to pursue legal action. Instead, he determined that the best approach was to attempt to negotiate another win-win compromise with the government—if the company survived. Just when the banks were ready to foreclose, an investor unexpectedly infused additional capital. The negotiations with the government's representatives continued, and while they remained unwilling to provide relief on the contract it had broken, they did promise Energy Equity (by this time renamed to Energy World) additional power plants in the future.

As the Indonesian economy rebounded and started to grow once again, Energy World's share price increased from one cent per share in 2004 to $1.40 by mid-2005. Suparno then decided to sell the family's shares and recoup 60 percent of their original investment when the stock price hit 20 cents per share, but the company did not allow him to do that because he served on Energy World's board of directors. By the time Suparno was allowed to sell, the share price had hit 60 cents per share, doubling his family's original investment. By the time the family completed their sell-off of the stock in 2005, the per-share price had hit $1.40. The large gain on their investment enabled the family to pay 100 percent of their more than $10 million severance obligation that resulted from shutting down their timber businesses and to repay all of their remaining debt. Suparno said,

> The miraculous combination of the positive results of the bank and Energy World negotiations with the government, the unexpected additional capital investor in Energy World, and the resulting gain we achieved when we sold our Energy World stock enabled us to pay off all of our obligations and debt and consolidate our businesses into a smaller, more synergistic group of companies. This series of events, when added to the liquidation of the timber and related businesses, was financially and emotionally traumatic, but the family made all of the decisions together and were never divided.

Suparno added that the family came out of this potentially devastating time as a stronger unit with their reputation intact, "a true blessing from God."

Bigger Is Not Always Better

In another unexpected chain of events, one of the family's public companies, Resource Alam Indonesia, diversified in 1998 by purchasing a coal mine in Indonesia. When the adhesive business was closed in 2005 as they transitioned out of the timber business, Resource Alam began expanding its coal-mining operations and supplying other countries, including China. The timing couldn't have been better as China's economy was growing meteorically, much of which was fueled by coal. By 2006, the family had three Indonesian coal-mining operations in Simpang Pasir, Gunung Pinang, and Bayur. In 2011, Resource Alam was recognized by *Forbes* as a "Best of the Best" company in the Asia Pacific region with sales revenue under $1 billion. Shortly after receiving the award, the company's market capitalization almost reached $1 billion—a dramatic difference from when its market capitalization had dropped to less than $10 million following the financial crisis.

Yet, by 2017, that market capitalization dropped back down to $176 million because of steep commodity price declines. Suparno said with a wistful smile,

Such is life in the commodity business. When you are rich, don't be arrogant, and when you lose most or all of it, don't be sad.

Because Resource Alam carries no debt and operates ultra-efficiently, it continues to be a profitable holding for the family and its other shareholders, even at that much-lower market capitalization.

Furthermore, as the family liquidated their timber-related businesses and paid off debt, they began investing more heavily in Global Palm Resources, their palm oil business. They now have four palm plantations in the Kalimantan region of Indonesia, comprising a land bank of over 40,000 hectares (98,800 acres), of which 43 percent is under cultivation with over two million palm fruit trees. These plantations are run highly efficiently and sustainably. Each hectare (2.47 acres) contains about 140 palm trees, each of which produces approximately 20 tons of fruit annually. The fruit is harvested every 10 days, and the oil is extracted within 24 hours of harvesting, consistent work that provides tremendous employment opportunities for people in the surrounding communities. Suparno said,

> We discovered the hard way that bigger isn't always better when you have to borrow heavily to grow. The consolidation allowed us more time and energy to seek and follow God's will and timetable regarding how to rebuild our businesses. It also enabled us to retain the best of the best non-family employees to serve and grow the businesses.

Even though the size of the company is smaller now, the family's net worth has remained about the same. All of the companies operate either with zero or very little debt.

Currently, Suparno and his family have three public companies: Resource Alam (Indonesia), Harrison Holdings Limited Berhad (Malaysia), and Global Palm Resources Holdings Limited (Singapore). The family owns approximately 70 percent of each. They also own private companies in three industries: real estate and real estate development, timber in China, and energy in Indonesia, primarily in hydroelectricity plants. All of the family shares are held in separate holding companies, one for each public and private company, which the seven second-generation family members own equally. If a second-generation family member desires, he or she can sell his or her interest in the holding company back to the holding company; in turn, this increases the remaining family-member owners' shares. The five brothers all run separate family businesses and are paid the exact same salary. Most of the brothers' compensation is derived from dividends distributed by the various holding companies.

Third-generation family members are welcome to work in the family businesses, and they are paid based on their responsibility and contribution to the success of the company.

The family is structuring the business and reporting accountability so that the companies can continue to be successful-

ly operated into the future through a combination of professional management and family members. Suparno said this is a priority and that their third-generation family members are

>...all very sensible in the management of money.
>Their sense of responsibility is quite good, and there
>is no entitlement mentality, pride, or arrogance
>among them.

There is also zero tolerance for corruption. Suparno said,

>We have a whistle-blower policy and encourage
>employees to use it to help us fight corruption. We
>also have accounting and accountability procedures
>dedicated to preventing and/or catching any acts of
>corruption.

Finally, each company's board of directors has a committee
that oversees their respective company's accountability policies
so that, as Suparno says, integrity is not compromised for money or for any other personal or corporate gain.

God's Timing

The family businesses have not only survived but were restruc-
tured in a manner that enabled them to thrive. Suparno said,

>God cleared the path for me and my family to end
>up with a business structure through which we
>could better serve Him. We could have never imag-
>ined or achieved this outcome, or anything close to
>it, on our own. Our role was to seek God's will and
>then patiently, humbly, and obediently follow
>where He led us. It took almost ten years, which
>seemed like an eternity, but in His time, He led us to

a much better place than we could have ever taken ourselves on our timetable.

Through the many ordeals and frightening times, Suparno never wavered in his trust in the Lord. He was faithful in prayerfully seeking God's direction and clarity and then patiently working through the issues as he was led. He strived hard not to compromise his biblical values even as the world around him was surrendering to corruption in the name of survival. He said,

> My faith and obedience to God's will grew stronger day by day, even as everything seemed to be falling apart and lost. It became clear to me during this time that, if you truly believe that God owns it, you have a responsibility to steward whatever He has provided with great care—whether that be a one-person business, profession, job, marriage, family, or multinational companies. I also learned that, if you truly believe God owns it, then it becomes easier to raise up and empower other people to serve and grow the business as ministry.

Two other experiences heavily influenced Suparno's perspective and path regarding his family business as his ministry.

First, in 2005, after a decade of managing the crisis-driven transformation of the family-business holdings, Suparno's faith was soaring. He agreed to host an event for Crown Financial Ministries to help pastors and business people learn biblical principles for stewardship of their money and other resources. He committed to Crown to have 500 pastors and 500 business people participate in life-changing events in Surabaya, Indonesia. He woke up one night shortly thereafter in a cold sweat, unsure of how he could accomplish such a lofty goal.

Suddenly, Suparno was struck with the realization that God owned the event, not him, and all he had to do was seek and follow God's instructions. He calmed down, prayed, and went back to sleep. The next day, Suparno immediately set in motion a strategy to form the right team to help him plan and execute the event. Suparno and Crown were elated when 900 pastors and 1,100 business people participated in the program. He said,

> Ever since then, I have understood that, if God owns it, then it will never fail, even if the result is different from what I expect. I can now do much without stress and sleep very well at night! It gives me an indescribable peace to know when I am serving God faithfully that, no matter what, everything will be okay because God will provide—and that His timing, while not always on the same schedule as mine, will be perfect.

Subsequently, Suparno joined a group of nine other local business owners in Jakarta for an intensive 10-day program conducted by Brett Johnson's Institute for Innovation, Integration & Impact. The program, called Venture, is designed to help participants repurpose their businesses to positively impact society using both marketplace and biblical best practices. It highlights four "ships":

1. Ownership (God owns it—not us.);
2. Partnership (We work together with Christ, but we are junior, and He is senior.);
3. Leadership (Christ is the CEO, and we should always seek and follow His lead.); and
4. Stewardship (Our job is to be good stewards and serve the owner's [God's] purpose.).

The Venture program helped Suparno more fully understand how he could productively serve God and others through his businesses. He became a leader for the program in Jakarta and ultimately helped train and mentor many business owners in repurposing their businesses.

Providing Education

While Suparno was immersed in the mid-1900s with God redirecting the path of the family businesses, his wife See Mun was busy following the Lord down her own new path. She felt her children could not find a good preschool education in Indonesia that suited her expectations, so See Mun decided to start a preschool for her children. To establish her credibility, See Mun pursued and achieved a master's degree in education in 2001-02.

Again, the timing was key. During Indonesia's recovery following the riots and economic collapse in 1998, the Indonesian government was broke and decided to deregulate the schools. After three years of praying fervently for the right opportunity, in 2001, See Mun seized the opportunity to pursue a major undertaking—the licensing of a private, Christian primary school. The Ichthus School was founded in Jakarta of which See Mun is the founding director and remains actively involved. It eventually expanded to two primary schools, two secondary schools, and two high schools. See Mun and Suparno also operate six franchised kindergarten locations. In all, they serve over 1,200 students in Jakarta with Christian education.

The schools are See Mun's passion and ministry, and it was through her that Suparno also discovered his fervor for education. As a result, he created a program for post-high school advanced certification acquisition and ongoing training. He said,

> This program focuses on helping students acquire international certifications like the Certified Financial Planner (CFP®) program that require lifetime continuing education once received.

They are currently working with over 100 universities and colleges of higher education serving over 40,000 students each year, and the graduates of the various programs have been increasing at a rate of over 40 percent per year.

Kingdom Entrepreneurship Academy (KEA)

In 2011, Suparno integrated everything he had learned scripturally in business and in education to become the co-founder of the Kingdom Entrepreneurship Academy (KEA). Its goal was to address three practicalities that he felt necessary for a Christian entrepreneur.

1: Enhanced skill training

KEA expanded the training program to six months, meeting two days every week for five hours each week. During the six-month training period, each student writes either a business plan for a new business or a plan to grow his or her existing business with the help of facilitators and other students. The studying and working together bonds the students into a close fellowship with one another.

2: Building community and accountability

KEA keeps the groups together after the initial six-month program is completed to learn, grow, and support one another; share challenges and ideas; participate in small-group studies together; and pray for and encourage one another.

3: Increased real-life experience

Successful Christian business owners are brought in to share their experiences and speak from the heart about how they apply biblical principles within their respective businesses. KEA also connects each student with a Christian business owner mentor. There are also plans to expand the program to include a Christian business incubator to help the graduates start businesses and an accelerator program that will bring successful business owners to consult and pray with KEA graduates who are having problems in their business, teach about capital acquisition, and discuss growth models.

***

In the process of developing and implementing The Entrepreneur Path, Suparno learned that his greatest passion is teaching and mentoring young people from their early 20s until age 40. "I must be a slow learner," Suparno said with a grin. "It took God a long time to bring me to this place."

Marissa Maren, who works with her uncle and cousins in the family's garment business in Jakarta, was in KEA's first graduating class. She said,

> The purpose of KEA is to create a new center in your life, one that honors God and builds His kingdom. Prior to KEA, I felt isolated as a Christian and not sure how to practice my faith. In Indonesia, the business is the center, and faith is for one day a week. I knew instinctively that this was not right.

Maren believes the program has benefitted her

> ...by providing a like-minded community of peers to whom I can go with challenges, issues, and doubts; helping me fully give my heart to God; and teaching me the integrity between my heart and my motives. It isn't just about trying to live according to biblical principles. The motives behind what I am doing are what God cares about.

I now understand that God is the owner of everything and I am called to be His good and faithful servant. Knowing this takes a huge burden off of me as I know He will provide for me and help me fulfill the purpose for which He created me if I trust Him and seek His will and help. My life has been much more fulfilling and much less stressful since I participated in KEA.

Core Values

The overriding objective in all that Suparno does in his businesses is to live his life and run the companies according to biblical principles. He said,

> This objective is not diminished within our public companies because our non-family shareholders appreciate our corporate values, and they make a good return on their investment. Being public also enables us to expose others to our faith through our stated core values, which are the same for all of our companies.

Those core values are as follows:

- **Stewardship**: Caring for God's property, people, and planet while earning a fair profit. Taking what God has provided and managing it faithfully.
- **Community**: Working in a collaborative spirit internally with our employees and their families, and externally within the communities where we conduct our business.
- **Partnership**: Partnering with our employees, the communities where we conduct our busi-

ness, our suppliers, the local and country's government, and those to whom we sell product to achieve shared goals and mutual benefit.
- **Commitment**: To integrity, excellence, and the other three core values.

An example of these core values in action is the work of Global Palm's and Resource Alam's Vice President of Sustainability, whose job is to focus on environmental sustainability (property and planet) and corporate social responsibility (people) as well as to recommend and help implement programs to improve the short-term and long-term impact on the communities in which they are located. This priority takes the form of investing in the communities around their plantations and mines to build community centers and schools, as well as medical centers with airstrips for emergency transportation and other necessities as determined by each community.

Helping Local Farmers

Suparno's companies go into areas where the land was previously unproductive and invest in and develop the land for use as a palm plantation. They then sell land leases to local farmers around their plantations at attractive prices. They teach the previously impoverished local farmers how to plant and maximize palm tree production and keep the land productive. They purchase the farmer's fruit, and once the loan for the lease is repaid, the farmer can then build personal wealth. They currently have approximately 3,000 families benefitting from this program and working their way out of poverty. They also provide educational scholarships to promising local students.

A strategic byproduct for Suparno and his family from living their core values and following biblical principles is that land owners and those in the surrounding communities desire to work with them. They have their choice of the best areas and locations in which to operate, and as a result, keep their costs low. Lower costs contribute to their higher return on investment, which enables them to invest more back into their communities and still have a better bottom line than their competitors. Suparno insists that their scriptural, long-term view enables their values-driven approach to be successful. "While we may not know where the path is going to take us during our earthly life," he said, "we trust and know that, with God in control, it will be excellent!"

Gratitude and Joy

Through their core values and the manner in which they honor them, Suparno believes he and his family are directing others to God. He said,

> Our core values are practiced in every company by every employee, Christian or not. They enable us to work across all religions and denominations, and even those with no faith, to build up others in things eternal.

Interestingly, only one of Suparno's four brothers are Christian, yet they and the other non-Christian employees buy into and live the core values because they have experienced firsthand their beneficial impact. He said,

> My purpose is building up others and clearing the path for them, just as the path has been cleared for me, so that ultimately I will be able to point them to the excellency of Christ.

He recalls a Bible verse that he believes sums up his lifetime journey to date: 1 Peter 2:9.

But you are a chosen race, a royal priesthood, a holy nation, a people for his own possession, that you may proclaim the excellencies of him who called you out of darkness into his marvelous light. (ESV)

Suparno explained,

I have personally experienced God's loving grace in Jesus' horrendous suffering and death on the cross to pay the price for my sins and in God's provisions for me and my family during and after the financial crisis. It is with the deepest gratitude that I am driven to serve and be obedient to God.

Suparno has no idea where he or his family's businesses would be today if he had not encountered God on that flight from Pontianak to Jakarta and not subsequently sought, trusted, and followed Christ down the path that had been cleared for him.

It is now with heartfelt gratitude and joy that Suparno clears the path for others, especially young people, leading them to the life that Christ desires for them. After all, unlike any earthly route, Suparno has experienced and understands that God's path benefits those who follow Him with blessings now and with eternal life to come.

Personal Reflection and Group Discussion

1. Suparno has numerous Bible verses to which he refers to help him deal with different circumstances, including his life verse. What Bible verses are most meaningful to you? Why? Do you have a life verse?

2. In very difficult situations that could have had devastating consequences, Suparno made a conscious decision to trust God and His promises no matter the outcome. How can you prepare yourself to be able to do the same when unforeseen difficult circumstances come your way?

3. Suparno said, "It is with the deepest gratitude that I am driven to serve and be obedient to God." What drives you to serve and be obedient to God?

4. How can you begin to seek God more often in prayer? Like Suparno, how can you benefit by journaling His responses to your patient intercession and obedience?

5. Suparno said, "I learned that life is not a dot—but an eternal line. Not 70 to 80 years here on Earth—but eternity." How does his statement change your perception of your purpose?

6. What other spiritual, business, and personal concepts and practices noted in this chapter stood out to you? How will you integrate them into your life and/or business?

7

GETTING TO THE
HEART OF BUSINESS:
SUCHY MESSTECHNIK

Lichtenau-Garnsdorf, Germany

THE YEAR WAS 1984, and 24-year-old Frank Suchy's life was about to take an unexpected and remarkable course-altering turn.

Frank was raised in the German Democratic Republic (GDR), also known as communist East Germany. The GDR was formed in 1949 out of the Soviet Occupation Zone following World War II when Germany was essentially split into two distinct and separate countries. West Germany retained its freedom and capitalistic roots, while the GDR, including half of Berlin, fell under the rule of the Socialist Unity Party, which made teaching Marxism-Leninism and the Russian language compulsory in schools. Both of Frank's parents, Wolfgang and Engeborg, were born and raised in the eastern part of Germany and had no family in West Germany. Wolfgang and Engeborg were only nine years old when the war ended, so their perspective of the world was limited to what they knew and experienced living under the rule of the Socialist Unity Party.

Frank, born in 1959 in Karl Marx Stadt, GDR, likewise grew up knowing no other way of life, and, compared to those around him, he felt his family was well off. Frank's family did, after all, have a small but adequate rented flat, a TV, refrigerator, and a washer and dryer. Frank's father was employed in a company that built textile machinery throughout Communist Eastern Europe. Frank described his childhood world as "materialistic," but not in the same way most people think of materialism. Rather, it was one dimensional, focused on what they had or could realistically expect to attain within the system under which they lived. The dimension of faith, and the love, hope, and joy it fosters, was virtually non-existent. Frank's parents, and most of those raised in the GDR, did not believe in God.

Wolfgang was mostly an absentee father to Frank as his job took him away from home three months at a time. When Wolfgang was home, Frank recalled that his parents often argued, and he never felt love from his father. Though Frank's mother was loving, his longing for his father's love never abated. "I grew up in an atheist world with atheist thinking," Frank said, "but I seemingly missed nothing except the good relationship with my father."

By 1984, Frank was still living in Karl Marx Stadt, a blue-collar town that is today called Chemnitz. Having served the mandatory 18-month stint in the military, Frank was comfortably settled into his government-approved work as a mechanic for textile machinery. He was well thought of within his company and was entrusted to educate and train new employees in repairing the machinery. He was also completing a five-year study at an institute-technical school in Dresden, GDR. During the program, Frank traveled nearly 60 kilometers (approximately 38 miles) by train once every month from Karl Marx Stadt to Dresden and back for a day of classwork. After writing a thesis, he would graduate and become a mechanical engineer with additional education for teaching. This would enhance his vocational route within the strict communist regime. From Frank's perspective, his career path was set—and life was good.

Course Correction

Then he met Birgit, the chance happening that placed Frank's course-altering change into motion. Interestingly, he credits Muammar Gaddafi, the former Libyan dictator for over four decades, with his and Birgit's fortuitous meeting and subsequent marriage. Erich Honecker, then GDR General Secretary, had a friendship with Libya's leader, and Germany was respected worldwide for how well it educated and trained its industrial workers. Because of the relationship between Gaddafi and Honecker, many Libyans were sent to East German companies for mechanical education and training, including Frank's company. One day, one of Frank's colleagues who trained the Libyans became ill, and the director of the school asked Frank to step in for him. Frank's assignment was to go to the lab and teach them to measure the calibration of the length. Birgit happened to work in that lab.

"I saw her, and I thought, 'Really nice! I will ask her out for a cup of coffee.'" She was shy, but, fortunately for him, the training in Birgit's lab took an entire week. While they acknowledged one another, Frank wasn't sure how to properly approach her for a date. He called her every night but couldn't muster the courage to ask her out. Finally, at the end of the week, and with time running out, Frank asked, and she enthusiastically accepted. He later took her to a restaurant in Karl Marx Stadt famous for its coffee and cake. They had a great conversation and recognized they were attracted to one another.

Then came something Frank couldn't possibly have anticipated from the timid young woman, though later Birgit explained, "If we were going to start a relationship, I felt I should show my cards." In the middle of their date, Birgit declared, "I must tell you something. I am a follower of Jesus."

Smitten with her from the moment he laid eyes on her, Frank wasn't prepared for this moment. He had met a few Christians over the years and heard about their Jesus who was born on Christmas Day and died on a cross. He also observed that they seemed to have something he might like. As an atheist, however, he had no idea how to access it and no knowledge of the Bible. So, not knowing what to say, Frank simply paused, looked her in the eyes, and said, "Okay." He then continued their prior conversation.

Birgit was one of a small percentage of the GDR population born into a Christian home. She and her parents lived with her grandparents in a home that had been in the family for generations. Located in the village of Garnsdorf, the home was in a rural agricultural area similar to the farming regions in Ohio and Pennsylvania. Birgit's father worked in the same company as she and Frank, but neither her father nor Birgit talked about their faith at work. To do so was strictly against the rules. Those known to be Christians were limited in the jobs they could have and could never hold a supervisory or teaching position.

Birgit did not know many committed Christian men her age, and it was unlikely that Frank or any other young, single, atheist in the GDR would choose to become a Christian. Yet Birgit was not willing to compromise her faith, even at the risk of never marrying or having children. She was worried that if she married a non-believer, she could eventually lose her faith. "I knew that it would be hard to go the way of Jesus if my husband was against it," she said, adding that it'd also be difficult to raise her children in the faith she loved without her husband's support. "It was very important for me to let Frank know that I was a follower of Jesus on the first date because, if he wanted to continue to date me, he would have to come to know Christ."

Following their date, Frank didn't contact Birgit for over a week. Birgit was certain the newborn relationship had ended faster than it started. But Frank hadn't abandoned her. He was thinking.

"What should I do with this?" Frank recalled thinking. "Birgit's commitment was really strong. She knew that if I never accepted Christ as truth, I will be the loser." Finally, Frank called Birgit and explained that he needed more time to think, then he asked how they could move forward. When asked how she felt at that moment, Birgit shared, with a huge smile and arms waving in the air, "Yahoo!" then added, "We started with small steps. I started taking Frank to church and introduced him to my pastor."

Just a few days after that, Frank said he was riding his motorcycle up and down hills and alongside streams through the rural countryside when the bike suddenly broke down. On the long and tiring nine-mile walk that followed, Frank began to talk to the Lord. "I asked, 'God, are you real? If so, show me.'" Later, he met with Birgit's pastor again and

> ...suddenly, something began to open up in me. The pastor had a special relationship with God, and he and I became friends. He understood that I was a thinking man, so he gave me books to read at exactly the right times that addressed my questions and thoughts.

Frank said one book in particular, about how the Bible was written, was significant.

> The book pointed out that the Dead Sea Scrolls, which were found in in 1946, proved that what was written in the biblical book of Jeremiah was true. It also helped me understand that all the prophesies in the Old Testament were written long before the fulfilling events actually occurred. My prior atheist mind would have assumed that the Old Testament prophesies were written and inserted into the Bible after the events actually happened to make it look like prophesy was fulfilled.

God continued speaking to Frank through his analytical intellect, and Frank also asked Birgit and her pastor lots of questions. He devoured the books her pastor gave him, and he bought a Bible and started reading it fervently. With every word he read, Frank was amazed how it all tied together. One day, Frank was pondering a spiritual question and arbitrarily opened his Bible to John 20:29, where Jesus tells Thomas, "because you have seen me, you have believed; blessed are those who have not seen yet have believed" (NIV). This was the first time Frank felt God's authority over him—an important key for him that confirmed how Frank's old, atheistic thinking was growing weaker and his new faith-driven thinking was growing stronger. He points out that the process wasn't easy.

> It is like going into the water for the first time. All of the safety points in your life are no longer in reach, but new, safer knowledge and capabilities are growing stronger. You just don't know yet if you can trust them.

Ultimately, Birgit brought Frank to church for a special event that her mother also attended, to introduce him to her. Later, Birgit's mother conveyed that she thought Frank was a nice man and gave her daughter a "thumbs up." Frank and Birgit dated for one year and three months before getting married, during which time Frank came to know and accept Jesus Christ as his Lord and Savior. In the GDR, engaged couples were married by the government. They showed up at the government office at 9:00 one morning and baffled the workers present by refusing to exchange rings. But the government employees didn't know Frank and Birgit were going to exchange rings later that day when they officially consecrated their marriage in their church.

Accomplishing the Impossible

Now living a new life as a married man and as a born-again Christian, Frank realized his faith conflicted with totalitarianism. At the suggestion of three of his colleagues, Frank decided to start his own company. One by one, he diligently shared his desire with the owners of 32 companies in the GDR. Knowing how difficult it was in East Germany to get governmental approval to launch a new business, all the owners laughed away his dream—except one, the 32nd and last business owner he persistently approached. That owner's company told Frank that his customers had to wait for up to two years to get pressure gauges serviced or repaired. He suggested that it would be great to have someone like Frank as a service partner who could fix or maintain the pressure gauges.

Seeing the opportunity he'd been waiting for, Frank contacted the government and said he wanted to start a new business servicing or repairing the gauges. The GDR official asked him where he currently worked, and Frank answered the question, adding that he was also training workers there. The official then said Frank needed to first be released from his training duties at his current employer, and then he'd have to obtain a license from a higher level of the government to be allowed to start his new business.

"I wrote a letter to the company where I was employed, said that I had become a believer in Jesus Christ, and that the Bible was the basis and foundation of my life—and that was the reason I cannot educate people in communistic thinking," Frank said. He added to the letter, "If I build my own company and repair pressure gauges, maybe I can serve this country in another way."

That bold, daring letter resulted in Frank being removed from training the other employees. He retained his job but took a salary cut in the process. He called his choice "a way of no return," and everyone told him he was crazy. His father was more specific. "He came up to me and said, 'Do you know what you did? They will try and take away your engineering degree.' It was a very difficult time because only one person stood with me—my Birgit. She had the same spirit and same faith," Frank said.

> I closed a door that morning. But I had safety and peace in my heart. It was a feeling that I had never had in my life. Around me, everything was in trouble, but inside myself, I knew that it didn't matter what people say. This is God's way and I will do it! One advantage of being a Christian is that we have the certainty of God's way. This was a complete new experience.

Confident in God's direction for him to start his own business, Frank then sent another letter, this one to the higher authority within the government, asking for the license. In the meantime, he stepped out in faith and started purchasing material from the pressure gauge repair company to build the equipment he'd need to become their service partner. The higher level of government stated it would grant him the license for his own business, contingent upon him securing the service agreement with the pressure gauge company. A written agreement to move forward upon receipt of the permit was created, which satisfied the government—and after three months, license in hand, Frank achieved what God had led him to do. He launched his own business, *Suchy Messtechnik*, repairing and maintaining pressure gauges, in 1988.

For the next two years, demand for gauge repair remained steady. Then another unexpected turn came for Frank, Birgit, and everyone else in East and West Germany. On November 9, 1989, the spokesman for East Berlin's Communist Party announced that citizens of the GDR were free to cross the country's borders starting at midnight that day. Masses of people flocked to checkpoints all along the wall in Berlin that had separated east from west since 1961, as well as to other checkpoints between the two countries. They flooded through as the gates were opened. That weekend alone, an estimated two million people crossed the border. Many used a hammer and picks to tear away at the wall; others employed cranes and bulldozers. East and West Germany were united for the first time since the end of World War II. The reunification became official on October 3, 1990.

The momentous event had a more practical effect on Frank's fledgling business: people wanted new pressure gauges, not just repaired and maintained ones.

> I worked together with a producer of standard pressure gauges in the west part of Germany, and from our working place in Garnsdorf, I started the manufacture of our own new pressure gauges.

Much to Learn

With communism vanquished in Germany, Frank faced two challenges as a manufacturer: he had to develop the innovative technology needed to produce better gauges, and then he had to market them effectively. An even bigger dilemma for Frank, though, was how to be an entrepreneur while taking into account his Christian beliefs.

> I grew up in a communistic regime. Everything I learned and knew about economics was wrong. Now that I had economic freedom, I had to make my own decisions and know what was wrong and right. Was it right to have private production machines? To have personal money and capital?

Even basic issues such as why people are rich or poor, Frank now had to examine through his Christian worldview, not old communist rhetoric. Plus, he had no experience in an open, capitalistic system. No one did. "It was a real challenge for all people," he said.

Frank discovered Christians in Business (CIW), a German organization founded in 1902 in Berlin. A friend invited him to a weekend retreat where several speakers talked about the challenges of being a Christian in the business world.

> This touched me, I made friendships, and they invited me to their companies and they visited my company. They helped me to understand some topics, which was really helpful for me. I became a member of CIW and we started reading *Business by the Book*, written by Larry Burkett. Sometime later, CIW produced their own material to go along with *Business by the Book*, adding a lot that related to entrepreneurs in our culture.

As his involvement in CIW continued, Frank observed how much the German people had trusted in the fallen communist system. As information was released to the public showing the shortcomings of the former GDR government, Frank said it was too much for some people. "It broke their heart and their mind. A lot of them came to their own conclusion of no longer trusting anything or anyone. They were closed to the gospel as well," he said. Frank also observed that the Christian church in Germany also struggled with the political change. He noted that the church "was in a good situation" before the wall fell, but that afterward many fellow believers became distracted, "looking for new things they can buy." In essence, they were in church when they needed God. But when their prayers were answered and they were given freedom, some decreased their involvement in church and commitment to God to pursue things they never had access to before. "It's crazy," Frank added, "but it's true."

Frank watched this materialistic trend have a negative impact, too, on his entrepreneurial colleagues. "I saw so many friends and neighbors start their own business, and suddenly, they had a new BMW in front of their house. Later, many of them went bankrupt." This occurred, he observed, because several of their business grew too quickly. His business, on the other hand, expanded gradually. "This protected me, but I didn't know it. Our business slowly grew, which was the best possible way."

While he borrowed money from banks to help with that steady business growth, he did so conservatively and at a rate he knew *Suchy Messtechnik* could handle. "I have a good feeling what we can do and what we can't do. I think that's one of the secrets, and it's in safety. I like risks, but I have a feeling for what is too big of a risk," he said. The borrowed funds also allowed Frank to both have the equipment needed to produce the new gauges, and to keep more parts in storage so he could deliver his products in two weeks versus four to six weeks. This gave him a competitive advantage.

His sound financial planning yielded excellent results. Over the business' first decade, Frank established the company and its revenue. Since that time through 2016, the company's revenues have increased by 165 percent, with consistent growth each year. As it nears its 40th anniversary, *Suchy Messtechnik* has 15 employees, including Birgit and their son, Markus, who has worked at the company for 12 years and is currently the company's sales manager. Frank has kept his salary at a very modest level by developed countries' standards, making what a low- to mid-level manager would annually earn in the United States, and taking the rest of his compensation from the profits of the company.

Frank's role with CIW grew as well. He joined its board of directors in 2002 and served as chairman for five years until

2013. "This was a really challenging time because I learned how different Christians can be, and the challenges of walking spiritually with other Christians. Not only are there differing beliefs, but different desires of the heart. Some were working to please God; others were working to make a career for themselves. It was not always easy to recognize who was who," Frank said, adding that he learned much and benefited from his time with CIW. "It opened doors for me and made connections with people I would have never met," he said.

From there, Frank became involved with CBMC International (Connecting Business in the Marketplace to Christ). He took a lesser role on the board with CBMC than he had at CIW, after being encouraged by both Birgit and Markus to give more attention to his business, and remains on the CBMC board today. He found redefined purpose there and identified an effective way to positively impact other Christians that wasn't available to him at CIW in this way. "My vision is that entrepreneurs and appointed executives realize who they are in Christ and how they can perform their pastorate in the economy under the leadership of the Holy Spirit," Frank states on his CBMC biography page. "We become salt and light of the earth, as well as fathers and mothers, who support other people to embrace their calling and live in a lively relationship with Jesus Christ."

Success

Not surprisingly, Frank defines all his achievements through a distinctly biblical filter. "Success means for me to be in the way of God. It means that the things written in the Book of Life come alive on Earth. We are a small company; 'success' sounds so large. But the main success is creating an environment where people can grow and use their gifts, where employees can feel they are worthy as people and valued as workers," he said, adding that this requires him to be a trustworthy steward of the people God has given him.

I believe God's role is to give each of us a field at a size He decides, and we must be trustful laborers and stewards to work in this field like a farmer. But being the owner of a company is additionally like being a shepherd. What is the task of a shepherd? To care about the sheep. To guide the sheep to places where they can feed and drink. The shepherd doesn't have the sheep for his own benefit. He has to serve the sheep and afterwards he can live from the sheep. I must keep my word if I buy some goods from a supplier; I must pay the invoice on time. If I have an agreement with my employees, I must pay the salary on time. I think this is the basis for being a good steward.

On his *Suchy Messtechnik* bio page, Frank cites the values of his company as honesty, reliability, and kind and helpful relations with customers, and he says his company practices an active exchange with other enterprises in the Association of Christian Businesses. Professionally, Frank sees himself as a pioneer.

I like to step in new areas and new fields. I like to fix things and to say that we make things. I am really an engineer with a technical feeling and understanding. I can see in my mind what is going on inside pressure gauges. I can feel it. This is one of the gifts God has given me.

Life Motto

Frank proclaims his life motto as, "Bringing fruit through investing in people," and one way he's doing this is by teaching in his church on subjects such as faith, trusting God, and financial stewardship. He has a passion to deliver practical teachings to people to help them live as a Christian through everyday challenges. Another way Frank invests in people, and one he says is his greatest accomplishment, is by being a good father to Markus.

> We can travel together, we like to spend time together, and we like to work together. Not many fathers have this close relationship with their son. The secret is when Markus was a child, especially on the weekends, I spent time with him and we worked together on the garden and the house. I showed him how to do something, then let him do it afterward and supported him. Markus asks me things, and he doesn't have a problem when I see things from another perspective. I didn't blame him again and again like other fathers do to their sons, and that is why he can listen to me. He knows my heart for him. This is the secret, and it is so easy.

A third way he achieves his life motto is through a renewed vision for his business that Frank said God gave to him, Markus, and Birgit when they went to Silence House, a Christian retreat about 20 miles away from their home.

> We spent two days to talk about our vision and our desire, and which direction the company should go. The old vision for me was good products, motivated employees, and modern machines, and this goal was achieved. But now we want to be the most competent partner for our customers in the pressure and temperature gauge industry. The new vision is not product and machines, but how can we serve people the best way—and this belongs to my heart and gives me new motivation. That new motivation gives me new energy.

The little thing that makes a big difference in Frank's life—and the fuel for living out his life motto—is prayer.

> It is my time in quiet communication with God, sharing and listening and seeking His will, that makes all the difference in my day and my life. I literally get on my knees and seek God to help me.

Frank added that he especially likes to rest in silence before God and enjoy the presence of the Lord.

> After a while of doing this, your thoughts don't interrupt as often. This is really a key and a tool the Holy Spirit gave us against stress and all the noise in the world. It is written, "There is rest for my people," and we have to come to God in Spirit and in Truth. These belong together for me.

Frank is most grateful that God searched for him and loves him, saying many people try to reach out for the love of God, but that His love is already there because He loves us first. Frank recalled a pastor on God TV who recently asked his audience, "What is the worst thing that can happen to you?" Answers included getting cancer or losing loved ones, all devastating, but Frank said, "The worst thing that could happen to me is for God to take away His Holy Spirit from me." He can't fathom being separated from the Lord. Likewise, Frank's greatest joy comes from his relationship with God, who he calls "the provider of peace" who brings peace to his other main joy, his family. In terms of what he's most hopeful about, Frank points to the truth of the Bible.

> "The Word of God is the truth and is the basis for all my hope. Not only do I believe in it, but I have a lot of experiences to know that it is the truth. So many

times, I challenge people and say, "Try and read the Bible as written—try to do it and make small steps. And if you feel that this step is carrying you, you can make the next step, and the next step, and the next step." This is where faith is growing through experience.

It's no wonder, then, that Frank has several significant Bible verses, but he highlights three in particular. Considering his story, they fit perfectly with who Frank was, is, and is becoming as he daily lives out his faith in God:

- "Therefore, there is now no condemnation for those who are in Christ Jesus." (Romans 8:1, NIV)
- "And we know that in all things God works for the good of those who love him, who have been called according to his purpose." (Romans 8:28, NIV)
- "By wisdom a house is built, and through understanding it is established." (Proverbs 24:3, NIV)

"The most important thing," Frank adds, "is to trust God, and you will have personal experiences you never expected."

A New Venture

With that as motivation, Frank now feels compelled to share with other business owners the knowledge and wisdom that was, for him, "born out of pain and experience." Both were the result of learning things the hard way, making mistakes, and then keeping his faith and business progressing forward. To distribute his insights, Frank has started a publishing company called *Verlag Business gestalten,* which translated means, "Shaping Business."

> The purpose is to support entrepreneurs and business leaders to find their calling from God for their life—to realize why they are alive and why they are in the position where they are right now.

Through *Verlag Business gestalten,* Frank will take speaking opportunities and provide written and digital materials, including a weekly newsletter, to convey wisdom and experience that he believes will address the needs of business owners.

> They are working hard, and they really have a passion for their company or business they are doing, but they are very stressed. Many companies aren't organized well, and as a result, the owners don't see how they can take the time to have a really deep relationship with God. Even many of the professed Christian business people are not strong enough as Christians, which makes them unprepared for all of the business challenges they face.

In Frank's volunteer work over the years with many influential Christian business organizations in Europe, he has observed a common trend—they are not growing. In some cases, their membership is even declining. Frank wondered why these organizations aren't keeping up with the needs of business people if they are professing biblical principles. He concluded that in many cases, entrepreneurs are so stressed with the daily issues they face that they aren't willing to learn and practice the very principles from Scripture that will set them free from pressure and anxiety. "Many are like hamsters running on a big wheel," he said.

Frank is using the publishing company, its website, digital materials, and associated workshops and seminars, to approach entrepreneurs differently. He teaches them how to better organize their businesses so they will have more time and be less stressed, then he shows them how to use that time to deepen their relationship with Christ. The goal is for others to encounter the same peace in, and passion for, their business that Frank is experiencing. He is convinced that if he speaks to their needs as business owners and provides practical and immediately implementable solutions, believers and non-believers alike will continue to come and listen.

> This is where I will capture their attention, by addressing their challenges and needs. Once I help them solve their problems, I can then speak to their hearts. I have a message for Christians to strengthen them spiritually, and I have a message for those of the world because I walked in their shoes before I became a Christian. I know their feelings and language, and therefore can talk to their hearts and, I believe, bring them to Christ as well.

Frank adds that the key is to first help entrepreneurs become excellent at conducting their business, then encourage them to see that their business is their calling and that through their business, they can honor and serve God as they grow in relationship with Him.

> I understand the needs of the entrepreneur because they are the same needs that I had to address and fix to make my business run with excellence and to honor God. Now I can support and serve other business people and bring them closer to Christ. This is my calling. My heart is burning for this!

Ever since Birgit's bold declaration on their first date, Frank has been led on a journey from his atheistic life in communist GDR to a crossroad where he chose to open his heart and mind to the pull of the Holy Spirit. From that moment on, Frank's commitment to his faith and to prayerfully following God's will has resulted in him discovering and living the purpose for which God created him. Frank now knows that his pastorate is in the marketplace, serving other business owners and bringing them closer to Christ. For Frank, this is what it means to get to the heart of business!

Personal Reflections and Group Discussion

1. Before Frank believed in God, his analytical intellect had to be satisfied regarding his questions about Christianity. How has your intellect been satisfied concerning God? What do you still question about your faith?

2. Frank's future wife Birgit was willing to "show her cards" and risk never marrying by committing to wed a Christian only, which were then in short supply in communist East Germany. Are you willing to show your cards? What risk have you taken, or are willing to take, that reflects the depth of your faith?

3. After Frank became a follower of Christ, he realized that his faith and his profession were not compatible and that he needed to make a career change. Are you confident that you are living the purpose for which God created you through your current work? If not, what do you need to do to align your work with God's calling for you? Who can help you by holding you accountable?

4. Frank had no idea how to run a business, especially according to biblical principles. He sought help through an association of Christian business owners. There are many excellent Christian business resources available today. Have you sought the right resource(s) or organization(s) to help you run your business according to biblical principles? If not, create an action plan and timetable to do so and begin networking.

5. Frank said, "One advantage of being a Christian is that we have the certainty of God's way." What does that statement mean to you?

6. While not all his employees are Christians, Frank has built the culture of his company around his Christian values, and his employees respect and appreciate these values because Frank strives to live them faithfully every minute of every day. Is your company's culture aligned with your Christian values? If not, what do you need to do to get into alignment?

7. What other spiritual, business, and personal concepts and practices noted in this chapter stood out to you? How will you integrate them into your life and/or business?

8

ONE MORE: HOBBY LOBBY

Oklahoma City, OK, USA

WHAT COULD CAUSE A MAN to crawl under his desk so others couldn't see him pleading with God?

The year was 1986, and in David Green's words, nothing he tried had worked. He wasn't sleeping, and his nerves were shot. Every time the phone rang, he knew it would be another creditor wanting payment. The utility companies were threatening to cut off the water and electricity. When one bill or creditor was paid, another was delayed. He couldn't pay his vendors, and he found himself spending more time pleading with bankers for loans. His young business had lost almost $1 million on $25 million of sales the previous year. He owed his primary creditor $1.3 million.

That may not sound like much business debt in today's terms, but this was a business that David and a partner started in 1970 on $600 of borrowed capital. It was a business started by a man who repeated the seventh grade and didn't have a college degree. He said the only reason he graduated from high school was because the principal was "ready for him to move on." David Green had achieved a level of success no one could have imagined. But now, his company was bleeding to death. Everything he had worked for was collapsing around him.

Why had this happened to his business, Hobby Lobby?

***

David's father was a pastor in rural Oklahoma whose church had an attendance of around 35 regulars. His father's tiny salary was supplemented by the weekly "poundings" of the congregation in which food was brought to the altar so his family of eight could have something to eat. The family did not own a car. They wore hand-me-down clothes given to them by compassionate relatives.

High school was an uncomfortable place for David. It seemed like all the other kids had new clothes and plenty of money for snacks. David was the kid off to the side washing dishes in the cafeteria to earn money for a lunch pass. He had nothing new and no money. David became terrified whenever he was required to stand up and give an oral report in front of the class. He had once mispronounced the word "the" as "thuh," which his classmates thought was hilarious. They did not conceal their laughter. From that point, he simply froze in his seat when his turn came to stand in front of the class and present. If not for a kindhearted teacher who allowed him to come after class and give the report just to her, he would have failed the class.

His saving grace was Distributive Education (D.E.), more commonly known today as a work-study program. David earned class credit while going to work and earning income. On David's first day in D.E., at 10:30 a.m., he walked the mile from school to his future in retail. His first real job was at McClellan's five and dime on Hudson Street in Altus, Oklahoma.

That job at McClellan's led to a love of the retail industry and eventually to the five and dime chain, TG&Y.

Risk and Reward

David was working in management for TG&Y in Oklahoma City in 1970 when he and a friend, Larry Pico, began talking about starting a business. David's customers at TG&Y kept asking for small canvas art picture frames in his crafts department, but he had been unable to find a good supplier. David and Larry decided to go into partnership and manufacture and sell picture frames in their spare time. They combined their two last names to derive the company name Greco, a name and company that exists to this day as one of Hobby Lobby's manufacturing arms.

Owing their banker $600 was a huge step and even bigger risk as they had no spare money. This venture could break them. David, his wife Barbara, and their three small children—Mart, Steve, and Darsee—were living modestly but contently on his salary. David's prospects with TG&Y were bright. It was a growing company with what seemed like a secure future. Even so, David and Larry had confidence in their idea and a drive to own a successful business. David and Barbara also had no personal debt, which aided their prayerful decision to launch the business.

David and Larry invested the borrowed $600 in a foot-pedal-operated chopper to cut the wood for the art frames and an assortment of molding sticks, glue, clamps, and canvas. David and Barbara's small home only had a carport, so the chopper was set up in Larry's garage. Barbara glued the frames at their kitchen table during the day while David was at his day job. David and Larry helped at night and on weekends, and David's sons Mart and Steve even got into the operations, earning a robust $0.07 for each frame they glued.

David gave some frame samples to an enterprising salesman who called on David at the TG&Y store. Two weeks later, the salesman returned with a grin and $3,500 worth of orders from various retailers in Texas and Oklahoma. David and Larry were thrilled—until they realized they didn't have enough money to purchase the supplies necessary to fulfill the order. They asked their supplier to give them extended terms on their credit, and he did so because he believed in the two hard-working entrepreneurs. They made a $300 profit on the orders and invested it back into the business.

The business continued to grow and, within two years, they opened their first tiny retail store. It had 300 square feet for retail space in front and another 300 in the back that housed the "manufacturing" operation. A customer suggested the name "Hobby Lobby" for their new arts-and-crafts retail store, and the name stuck. Their rent was $250 a month, and in their first month, they grossed $136.17. Some days, there were no customers at all. But they worked hard, learned, and persevered. By the close of their second complete year of business in 1974, David and Larry grossed $150,000 and cleared a $36,000 profit. A 24-percent profit margin is unheard of in the retail industry—unless, of course, the owners and their family members are also the employees and not taking any salary. All the profit was again reinvested into the business.

The success, however, mandated discussions about what to do next. Over a cup of coffee at McDonald's one morning, David and Larry realized they weren't on the same wavelength regarding how to run and grow the business. David bought Larry out for $5,000 to the delight of both men.

By March 1975, David turned in his resignation at TG&Y. It was not an easy decision. He gave up a guaranteed salary of $26,000 a year with a seemingly secure $2 billion company. He was going to work as the bookkeeper, janitor, builder of home-made counters and shelves, and any other role that needed to be filled in this fledgling new company—for a salary of $13,000 a year. Many would consider this a step backward, not willing to subject themselves or their family to such a risk.

Yet David and Barbara had confidence in their dream and its opportunities. With prayerfully derived clarity, they decided to take the bold step. The Green family was now going to be fully committed to their enterprise with no "plan B."

Owning and building a business is difficult, especially in the early years. There are endless hours, lots of risk, and limitless challenges to overcome. But anyone who has ever owned a business, regardless of its size, knows that, when you are in this position, you need no motivation to get out of bed in the morning. And, at night, you usually fall back into bed exhausted and spent after a hard day's work. Each morning ushers in new hope, ideas, and enthusiasm.

Finding His Purpose...and Losing His Way

Though Hobby Lobby was successful, David couldn't help but feel like he was the black sheep of his family. He was the only one of six children who didn't follow their father into ordained ministry. David was not a good speaker or singer. He was uneasy with crowds. He seemed to have only one talent: making a retail store work properly. So that's what he kept doing.

He and Barbara went to church regularly and honored God in the way they lived. They taught their children to love God, and they strived to apply the Bible's teachings to how they conducted their business. For example, David turned down a lucrative offer to backhaul liquor in his empty trucks after store deliveries. It could have added $300,000 directly to Hobby Lobby's bottom line, a powerful boost for his fledgling company. But hauling the liquor wasn't compatible with his convictions. Yet his practice of applying biblical principles to all aspects of his life and business didn't alleviate his sense of being the black sheep.

That changed in the late 1970s. On a flight back from a church convention in Tennessee, a quiet but clear voice inside David urged him to give $30,000 for mission literature requested by one of the speakers during the conference. Of course, David didn't have the money and knew the company couldn't afford it. But in the days to come, the quiet, clear voice persisted—and David silently prayed.

An idea came to mind to write four checks for $7,500 each and postdate them a month apart for the next four months. He put the checks in an envelope, and with more faith than money, he mailed them off to Tennessee. When the church official called to acknowledge David's gift, he also shared a story.

> The very day your letter was postmarked was the same day four African missionaries had a special prayer meeting for much-needed literature funds. Looks like God answered their prayer!

Something ignited within David. God must have had a reason for giving him the talent to make a retail store succeed. Maybe God had a ministry purpose for a merchant like him after all. Perhaps the Lord had a place for the black sheep. David found his ministry as God's merchant-steward.

It wasn't easy, but David made adjustments as needed and was able to cover all four checks. The Lord had stretched David and his family in a new direction. They developed a deeper appreciation for sacrificial giving. David said,

> It was a black-and-white moment. I realized that our calling is our purpose and that our purpose has eternal value, directly or indirectly, through the people we touch. I didn't know if I was planting or watering, but I did know that I was where God wanted me. He called me to be a retailer.

By 1985, Hobby Lobby had grown from second-year revenue of $150,000 to revenue of $25 million. The business had been exceptionally profitable, and David and Barbara had given generously of their profits to ministries for which they had a passion, with the remainder plowed back into the growth of the company. They had believed and conveyed to whoever listened that the business was God's—not theirs. They had prayerfully and diligently tended to it daily.

Why, just one year later, were they on the brink of failure?

In the early 1980s, the oil industry boomed, and the regional economy in Oklahoma was vibrant. Money flowed freely, and luxury consumer items sold like hotcakes. The Rolex watch sellers and Mercedes Benz dealers couldn't keep enough inventory to satisfy demand. Hobby Lobby got caught up in the excitement and loaded up on all sorts of upscale merchandise such as high-end cookware, gourmet foods, signed and numbered artwork pieces, collector dolls, and the like.

When oil prices began to drop, energy companies laid off thousands of people, and a major bank in Oklahoma City failed. Simultaneously, the price of beef plummeted and hurt the state's cattle ranchers. Tax revenues skidded, and the state government tightened spending while passing the largest tax increase in its history. In his book, *More Than a Hobby*, David wrote that it was "almost as if I woke up one morning and the party was over."

He realized he had departed from Hobby Lobby's core business, arts and crafts, and had done so without making a careful or prayerful assessment. He also said that he had become prideful. David said he caught a wave and rode it, and in the process, he had made himself too big and God too small.

By 1986, the ride had ended with a crash. By then, all three children—Mart, Steve, and Darsee—were working in the business, as was Darsee's future husband, Stan, and two nephews, Jeff and Randy. David brought all of them together in his living room in April 1986, and for the first time, the family understood the gravity of the situation and the weight that David had been carrying for the entire family. They learned how he had been crying out to God for help from under his desk and during walks alone in Eldon Lyons Park.

Getting Back on Track

The family rallied around their dismayed husband and father. Barbara comforted David and reminded him that Hobby Lobby was God's business. The Lord would provide if He had other plans for them.

Mart reminded his father that their faith was in God. They would be okay even if the business was lost. He added, "Whatever happens, Dad, we love you."

Darsee's fiancé told David, "You're not responsible for our future. We'll make it somehow."

Through his family and their declarations of trust in God, David gained a peace that everything was going to work out one way or the other—as long as they continued to look to the Lord for direction.

David now understands that God was preparing him then for the future. He experienced firsthand where he could end up without God's help. His early success led him to rely too much on his own instincts and resources and not enough on seeking and trusting God's will and guidance. David vowed to never again take a risk or make an important decision without prayerfully discerning if his action was in alignment with God's purposes for him, his family, and his business. David learned that God cared more about his heart than his profits. He came to a new appreciation of Proverbs 3:5-6 and its declaration:

> Trust in the Lord with all your heart and lean not on your own understanding; in all your ways submit to him, and he will make your paths straight.

After a lot of what he called "praying like crazy," David and the family went to work reducing spending, extending credit, selling luxury items at deep discounts, and returning to Hobby Lobby's core business. With time, the business became a tree that produced significant profit—or, fruit. Half of that fruit was reinvested each year in new seeds to further grow the tree. The remaining 50 percent of the fruit each year was given to ministries. Surely, God was smiling.

Unfortunately, David was not.

Seeking Clarity

In the beginning, David's priorities were simple and remarkably profound. He wanted to build a happy marriage, raise healthy, well-balanced children who served God, and succeed in business. He had achieved all three, but now, David faced a new challenge, one almost as significant as when the business was on the brink of failure.

What am I going to do with all of this? he wondered.

It may seem like an odd question over which to agonize, but it weighed heavily on David's heart and mind. He sought counsel from Christian financial planners and attorneys whose advice on continuing the business and estate planning could ensure the business' viability, with the family benefiting and in control for generations to come. Yet David remained restless and relentlessly sought God's solution to his dilemma.

David's mind kept going back to what it means to be a good and faithful steward. A *steward* is defined as a person who is employed or appointed to manage another's property. "True stewardship starts with the realization that we owe everything good to God," said son Steve. "It is all His, and we were created to live and work for Him." If David and his family were truly appointed by God—or, in biblical terms, anointed by Him—to manage Hobby Lobby for Him, taking care of the family for generations to come, couldn't be the totality of the calling. How could they ensure that the business would always serve God's purposes?

To answer that question, the Green family turned to the Lord in prayer. It often takes immense patience to both seek and wait for clarity about God's will, but "clarity is God's job," David said. "Our job is to seek and then be willing to go wherever God wants—left or right, up or down." So they sought God, waited, and clarity finally came in three words: "Don't touch it."

"Don't touch it."

The Lord revealed that, if the Green family didn't own the business, it was not theirs to leave to future generations. The tree, Hobby Lobby, was God's. Their job was to care for the tree and then harvest and distribute the fruit, its profits, according to the Lord's will. The solution was not traditional but was spiritual with a literal application. They must lock up Hobby Lobby for God, protect the tree, and train themselves and future generations within the Green family to be faithful Christian stewards of its fruit.

While the opportunity to care for and grow the tree was to be passed down through the generations, the Greens also decided the tree itself would never be owned by family members. Therefore, the non-voting shares of Hobby Lobby and its affiliated companies were placed in a trust, the beneficiary of which is the Green Family Foundation. The 50 percent of annual earnings not reinvested back into the business each year were positioned to pour into the foundation. Likewise, if the business or any part of it is sold in the future, the proceeds would flow into the family foundation. The voting shares are owned and managed by the Green Stewardship Trust. This trust guides how the companies are to be managed. It also appoints the Board of Directors of Hobby Lobby Stores, Inc. The trust also has specific qualification requirements for its trustees aligned with the documented mission, vision, and values for the company. The trustees are responsible for ensuring that the right people are in the right jobs, family member or not, and that future leaders are trained to maintain and model the culture captured in the company's Statement of Commitments.

There are currently five trustees—David, Barbara, and their three children—and provisions allow for up to seven family member trustees. Each trustee has an equal vote. The Green Stewardship Trust was created to carry out the objectives of the settlors and to 1) honor God with all that has been entrusted to them; 2) protect, preserve, and grow the value of the Green family companies; and 3) use the assets of the Green Family Companies to create, support, and leverage the efforts of Christian ministries. Other guiding provisions are incorporated, including an exhibit with the trust's purpose, vision, mission, and values statement. A collaborative effort between the first and second generations of the Green family, the trust was well thought out with the help of a respected Christian advisor.

In all, three generations of Green family members are united in assuring that the business, foundation, and trusts will continue to serve God's purposes. The family understood that the starting point was to bring everyone together in unity and direction. David said,

> It doesn't do any good to dictate something that won't continue when you are gone. When everyone is together, the key becomes training those who are going to carry it on.

Training future generations to be committed and disciplined stewards, to love and serve the Lord, and hold firm to the trust's mission, vision, and values is no easy task. But David said, "If it's hard, I know it is ultimately going to be good."

David "Tyler" Green, David and Barbara's grandson and Mart and Diane's son, distinguishes the three generations of the Green family as G-1, G-2, and G-3. He said,

> The majority of the story is G-1 and G-2. First, grandpa. What amazes me is his simplicity and focus; the simple commitments he made as a young man. Then, how my dad and uncle have found their place and worked with grandpa to strengthen the biblical principle that it's not what you do but why and how you do it.

Tyler also cited Colossians 3:17:

> Whatever you do, whether in word or deed, do it all
> in the name of the Lord Jesus, giving thanks to God
> the Father through him.

He then added that the G-3 generation is forcing G-1 and G-2 to clarify and articulate those guiding principles for them and future generations. "That is liberating," he said.

Guiding Principles

The Green family functions according to guiding principles. The following are some examples and quotations that define how they steward the Hobby Lobby tree and its fruit.

1: Unity Around Purpose

The Greens worked with a non-family facilitator to help them collaborate and document their purpose and values in a Green family vision, mission, and values brochure. Woven with care, it professes the tapestry of the family's faith and commitment to intimate relationship with God, to loving family, and to serving others. Mart's business card declares the family's mission: "Love God Intimately. Live Extravagant Generosity." These two, three-word statements powerfully and clearly depict the family's calling. Steve said, "There is a common theme and practice in our family: trusting God." Mart added, "We practice doing the right thing—always—so when the game is on the line, we will know what to do."

The family's unity around purpose, trust in God, and commitment to never compromising their beliefs were put to an extreme test by the United States federal government passage of The Patient Protection and Affordable Care Act in 2010. A provision in the Act mandated that employers, regardless of their religious beliefs or moral convictions, were to provide insurance that would pay for four embryo life-terminating drugs and devices (also known as "emergency contraceptives"). For Hobby Lobby to do so, however, opposed the Green family's deeply held religious conviction to operate their company in a manner consistent with biblical principles. But if they refused the government's order to pay for these drugs and devices, the company would incur extremely punitive federal government fines of up to $1.3 million *a day*. Hobby Lobby could have been devastated.

The three generations came together to decide what to do. They did not intend to dictate their employees' choices. If an employee wanted to purchase emergency contraceptives, they were free to do so out of their own pocket. The Green family simply did not want Hobby Lobby to pay for something that could end a conceived child's life. Steve said the family could have reasoned that it was the law of the land and avert the problem by submitting to the federal government's requirement. However, if they fought the government, God could either have delivered them from the problem or the business could have suffered immeasurably. "When you put God's will first," Steve said, "you approach everything with an open hand, both to give and to receive. It's not ours to hold on to."

Despite the potentially dire consequences, the Greens were unified in their unwillingness to compromise their belief in the sanctity of life and the country's constitutional right to religious liberty. They decided to take on the federal government and filed their lawsuit over the federal mandate in September 2012. God had prepared them to take on Goliath. "We had no choice. If we say we are Christians and don't follow God's words, we are taking His name in vain. It was in God's hands," Steve said.

It took 21 months for the case to work its way through the court system. Injunctions were sought to gain emergency relief from the oppressive fines, but they were denied. David immediately thought of Shadrach from Daniel 3:1-30. He knew they were in the fire, but he had a peace that God was there to protect them. Finally, a court injunction to delay the fines was obtained—one business day prior to the implementation of the daily $1.3 million fine. The Green family rejoiced, prayed, and waited.

Ultimately, the case, *Burwell v. Hobby Lobby Stores*, went to the United States Supreme Court together with the sister case of Conestoga Wood Specialties Corp. In June 2014, the Supreme Court ruled in favor of Hobby Lobby and Conestoga Wood in what is considered to be a landmark case that upheld the constitutional right for citizens to live their faith without the fear of interference or retaliation by the U.S. government. They had been delivered from the fire!

2: Unity Around Process

The Green family developed habits around simple and repeatable processes that foster humble communication. David said,

> To achieve and maintain unity of purpose, we had to have good and consistent processes. We had to make sure the family is together.

Mart added, "All conflict results from unmet expectations. The solution is humble communication."

The family has a monthly gathering where the entire family comes together to celebrate the lives of those having a birthday that month. Each celebrant is asked to share what is transpiring in his or her life, and the other family members then share what they love about the celebrant as a form of positive affirmation. The family is now 35 members strong, and David has built a home solely for family gatherings in the heart of their Oklahoma City headquarters and warehouse campus that will accommodate future family gatherings of 50 and more. It even includes a nursery for the babies. They also have an annual family celebration the first Saturday of every new year to celebrate their blessings, welcome new family members, and discuss and reaffirm their commitment to one vision, one mission, and the same values.

The Green Stewardship Trust monthly meetings accommodate two committees that report to and give recommendations to the trust. The Giving Committee decides what outside ministries will receive family foundation funds, and the Investment Committee decides how excess capital should be invested. The Green Stewardship Trust also oversees the Hobby Lobby Stores, Inc. Board of Directors to ensure the family's vision, mission, and values are achieved. Additionally, if there is a family member matter related to the use of funds derived from the business—such as a family member who wants to become an employee and have funds contributed to their college education—the trustees of the trust will make the final decision.

The Greens also conduct a monthly giving committee meeting using documented requirements regarding who can serve on the giving committee and how they are selected. The committee funnels family ministry giving requests to the monthly meetings. They are expected to describe the ministry and how it fulfills the family mission, vision, and values statement. Each committee member then tallies a dollar-amount vote between $0 and $500,000. Once the votes are cast and reviewed, a dollar amount is determined for each request. There are also several ongoing ministry commitments that receive much higher amounts—a select few in the tens of millions—that are also reviewed for impact on the family purpose with the size of the gifts increased or decreased accordingly.

Why is unity around these processes so important to the three generations of the Green family? They know that the key to multi-generational success is relationship and communication, first with their Heavenly Father and then with one another. They are dedicated to open collaboration and a desire to understand as well as to be understood. Tyler said,

The heart of the training is life on life with grandpa, my dad, and the entire second generation. It is their priority that their children serve the Lord, and helping the third generation do so is very intentional. The key is everyone feels loved and involved.

3: Unity Fostered by Leadership

Leadership, David said, "is heavy" and means taking responsibility—whether in business, marriage, or family. He continued,

> Somebody ultimately has to be responsible. Until you acknowledge you are the leader, you are not responsible.

For David, leadership is never about one individual.

> It's not about me; that's arrogant. It's about God's will. It's biblical. God set it up that way, with Him as the true leader.

David also believes leadership requires balance.

> You have to give up some of your authority in order to make people's jobs a fun experience. If they don't feel empowered, they're going to dread coming to work in the morning. They need a certain degree of freedom in order to feel they are making a difference.

At Hobby Lobby, the entire family works together to raise up other leaders in the company, in the family, and in the ministries with which they are involved. David said,

I'm not *the guy* in any of our ventures. It doesn't all depend on me. A leader is raised up, and then, it is their job to collaborate and lead us forward. Every endeavor must have a champion. If there isn't a champion, it won't go anywhere.

4: Unity Around Accountability

Each family member is held accountable for the value they add. They are also accountable to the documented family mission, vision, and values they helped create. This accountability creates peace, not pressure, because they have guiding principles and training in place to facilitate accountability. The Green family intertwines that accountability, supported by the principles and training, with unconditional love and acceptance in a manner that creates a peace that surpasses understanding (Philippians 4:7). The corporate executive team is also accountable for acting with integrity in all matters. There are no exceptions. They are of one mind on this and have total freedom to challenge one another to live up to the biblical standards that are espoused and practiced.

5: "Get the right person in the right job—family or not."

David insists that understanding this principle is as valuable as a master's degree. Committing to it without compromise, however, is easier said than done. David applied this principle as he hired and replaced several chief financial officers until he had the right person in place. It took a couple of years and was challenging for all involved. When asked if he'd consider compromising "just a little" to speed up the process, David replied, "I won't stop searching until I have the right person in the right job. It will make all the difference in the world." He eventually found that person, and the difference made was stunning. The person's work was exemplary, and he perfectly fit the culture of the company.

6: "If you want baseball cards, earn the money to buy them."

Mart tells of when he was nine years old and wanted to start collecting baseball cards. His friend's father was buying the friend's collection, but David refused to buy Mart's. Instead, David suggested Mart save and use the $0.07 per glued frame he and his brother Steve were earning to buy the cards. Mart followed his father's advice and spent some of his earnings on baseball cards.

Later, Mart bought his own car and paid for his college courses. A lifestyle habit had been established, and at the age of 19, Mart was positioned to step away from his job at Hobby Lobby and pursue his dream to launch a new retail company. That company, Mardel Christian and Education Stores, now has 35 locations across several states.

The principle is basic and profound: If you want to make money in the Green family business, you have to earn it. There are always opportunities for family members who are capable and interested in working in the business to earn a fair and reasonable income. Each salary is earned according to their level of contribution to the well-being and growth of the business. Furthermore, the Green Stewardship Trust states that a family member will never earn more than 1.5 times the amount of compensation and benefits others performing comparable services are entitled to receive. David capped his salary 12 years ago, and today, several officers of the company make more than him. Finally, there will be no entitlement or trust funds for Green family members except what individual family members may save from their compensation and leave to their heirs. Green family heirs will have to continue to earn the money to buy their own baseball cards.

Discovering Individual Callings

Beyond Hobby Lobby, the Green family has learned that each person in the family needs to be encouraged to find their individual calling and be passionately supported in pursing it. David's sons, Steve and Mart, and grandson, Tyler, have embarked on some remarkable undertakings.

While Steve currently contributes to the success of the business, he believes he also has been called to help the family build one of the most extensive collections of Bibles and Bible antiquities in the world. This collection has been brought together and made public in the largest and most comprehensive Bible museum anywhere. It is housed in Washington D.C. two blocks off the National Mall. The Museum of the Bible is creative and interactive to help visitors better understand the Bible's history, its story, and the positive impact on humankind when its principles are applied. A byproduct of this endeavor is a parallel curriculum being developed for schools. Steve wants every student to have the opportunity to learn about this remarkable book and its influence on the world.

Mart applies his unique ability to bring people together in various ministries. He used his gift of collaboration to lead the remarkable turnaround of a dying Oral Roberts University and even served for seven years as the chairman of the board of the school. "People trust me, and I trust them," he said. But Mart's gift is also being used in a massive effort to unite, on one digital platform, every organization in the world involved in Bible translation. This digital Bible library will provide immediate access to God's Word in every language on Earth. The effort is called "Every Tribe Every Nation," and when completed, the Bible will be readily available to over one billion people who do not currently have access to it in their native language. It's an enormous undertaking and an amazing link between an ancient book and modern technology.

After graduating from college, Tyler went to work in Hobby Lobby's candle factory. But Tyler found that he "came alive" when he had the opportunity to be "on the ground" with the ministries supported by the family business. The family needed someone to steward the giving process, and for a time, Tyler enjoyed working alongside the family to help guide their mission work. Is this Tyler's calling? He is not sure yet. He says the business itself is a ministry, and he is careful not to look past the business to do ministry elsewhere. "It is a powerful thing that there is mission and ministry in the business itself."

Other family members have also found that their calling is working directly with the ministries the family business supports. For David, he understands that he was born to be a merchant. He said,

> I know I was called and am anointed to do what I do. Just when I think all the plates are spinning perfectly... *Bam!* God leads me to an opportunity or a problem that is a difference-maker. It is the same thing for me six days a week, being the best merchant I can be.

Living biblical principles in all phases of life and business led David to make decisions that were different than he might have made otherwise—writing, postdating, and mailing four checks in the amount of $7,500 each when he had no idea how to cover them; not hauling liquor when it could've made thousands; taking a stand against the U.S. government to preserve the sanctity of life and religious liberty at a risk of a $1.3 million daily fine. Most would consider these to be poor business decisions, but when it comes to combining business economics and honoring God, David insists, "You can't get there with a calculator." Regardless of popularity or their ability to contribute to profit, items that are not consistent with the family's convictions are not sold in Hobby Lobby stores. Cigarettes, ash trays, shot glasses, or risqué greeting cards are nowhere to be found. Alternatively, Hobby Lobby invests in character training for its employees, provides them with a free medical clinic, and brings in full-time chaplains with counseling backgrounds to help employees with personal issues.

Promoting the Reason for the Season

David made two other notable decisions based on his Christian faith that went against business spending norms. David was flipping through the newspaper one Christmas morning when an odd question disturbed his consciousness. *Why did that day's issue have nothing to say—not a single word—about the birth of Jesus Christ?* There were plenty of expressions of "Seasons Greetings" and "Happy Holidays," but that was it. The family discussed a new advertising approach. Nobody was talking about the real meaning of Christmas or Easter, days that were extremely significant to them both spiritually and as merchants. The Greens decided to be bold and share what the days truly mean.

Their first ad ran in all of their stores' markets for Easter 1997. The text of the ad showed a crown of thorns and said,

> For God so loved the world he gave
> acceptance
> peace
> mercy
> confidence
> purpose
> forgiveness
> simplicity
> hope
> relief
> comfort
> equality
> life

his Son.

This Easter we encourage you to believe in the love that sent Jesus Christ.

Accept the hope. Accept the joy. Accept the LIFE!

Hobby Lobby Stores Inc.

Since then, Hobby Lobby has run a new full-page ad every Christmas and Easter and features a gallery of these ads on their website.[3]

Closing on Sundays

In 1998, the Green family chose to begin closing their stores on Sundays. This made no business sense. Sundays are an outstanding day of revenue for retail businesses in America, and Hobby Lobby's annual Sunday earnings was $100 million. But David and his family felt convicted to allow their employees time every Sunday for family and worship. The store's sales volume and profits initially took a dip, and the banks were more than a little nervous because, at the time, Hobby Lobby still borrowed a lot of money to power its growth. Then, an amazing thing started to happen. Sales volume began to increase. By the close of 2001, Hobby Lobby experienced the highest percentage of profit in its history. "Once we did what we were supposed to do, profits took off," David said, adding that the employees' response to Sundays off "continues to be ecstatic!"

Raising the Company's Minimum Wage

In 2009, David once again asked himself, "So what else can I do to serve the Lord?" God led him to think about his first-level employees, many of whom were single mothers. The minimum wage they were qualified to receive was not sufficient, forcing many to work two jobs to support their families. The Green family decided to raise the minimum hourly wage they were paying new employees, first from $7.25 to $10.00 and then increasing it by one dollar every year from 2010-2014. By 2015, the company's minimum wage was $15.24 an hour. Since then, this has been adjusted yearly for inflation so that no employee's wages will ever decrease in buying power. Each wage increase costs one-half-of-one percent to the bottom line. But once again, the employees are thrilled.

Many employees have been able to drop their second job and have more time with their family. As a result, employee turnover has decreased substantially, and Hobby Lobby is able to attract and retain the best of the best hourly workers.

Hiring Practices

A person isn't required to be a Christian in order to work at Hobby Lobby, nor is preference given to Christians. The family has set a positive environment based on biblical principles. They let their employees and others draw their own conclusions.

No Long-Term Debt

In 2009, Hobby Lobby finally reached the goal of having no long-term debt. Its growth is now fueled from internal cash flow, giving it a tremendous advantage compared to highly leveraged competitors who have to allocate a large amount of their earnings to debt service. The Green family can reinvest more of their earnings into growing the tree and also giving more to serve God's purposes, bearing fruit far beyond money.

"It's a matter of faith."

The family's Christian convictions weave through every aspect of the company. Their choices are not all about money. They are not short-term decisions. They are eternal at their core. David said,

> It is a matter of faith. I am convinced that, if we serve God and honor him in all we do, we will be blessed—although maybe not in the short term. Every time we find another area to apply God's principles and do the right thing, the more we grow.

When asked to identify the one little thing that makes the biggest difference, the 10 percent that makes 90 percent of the impact, David immediately responded, "Praying without ceasing throughout the day—thanking, acknowledging, seeking." For David, his prayers include business matters.

> There is a God, and He's not averse to business. He's not just a "Sunday deity." He understands margins and spreadsheets, competition, and profits. I appreciate the open door to discuss all those things with Him and to see what He can accomplish through ordinary retailing.

Mart added,

> Strong relationships are built on strong, humble communication. Our communication with God first and then with each other is the key to loving God intimately and living extravagant generosity.

What is the result of this commitment to prayer? Tyler said,

Communication isn't a gift that comes naturally. Our family recognized the need to take the time to communicate, be with each other, have fun together, ask questions of each other, support one another, and have shared purpose. It takes a whole different level of relationship to do so.

It is difficult to imagine the never-ending, day-to-day challenges of running a business the size of Hobby Lobby. Many would cave under the pressure. Being united in and committed to their guiding principles have enabled three generations of the Green family to work through numerous challenges and progress forward. It has required hard work and tireless tenacity, but it's been a labor of love that has flowed through the Greens' outstretched, open hands.

By the end of 2017, Hobby Lobby had approximately 800 stores and affiliated companies generating approximately $4.7 billion in revenue. They have about 37,000 employees and three different retail concepts: Hobby Lobby, Mardel, and Hemispheres. There will be over 150,000 total items in the stores and 10 million square feet of supporting warehouse space in Oklahoma City. They give away hundreds of millions of dollars to Christian missions through their foundation and reinvest an equal amount into the growth of the company.

The security of a $2 billion company that David thought he was leaving when he resigned in 1975 was an illusion. One company that was thriving is no more, while the counterpart that was started by a humble man with little education is now over twice its size.

"What are you doing for the Lord?"

So what continues to drive David to work six days a week with an urgency that seems as if his life depended on it? Why is he always digging for ways to improve the company and produce more profit when his margins are already off the charts? Why are his children and grandchildren likewise determined to en- sure that the family and company stay grounded in its purpose?

It started with David's mother. Whenever he proudly told her about a business accomplishment, she simply smiled and then quietly replied, "That's nice, Dave. But what are you doing for the Lord?" As David started becoming successful and ac- complishing goals, he used to ask, "Now what?" But he realized he needed to transition that sense of earthly success to one root- ed in scriptural significance. David, Barbara, their children, and their children's spouses expanded her question to ask, "So what are we doing to show the next generation what it means to live for Christ?" They desire to do everything possible to ensure fu- ture generations grow up to love and serve God.

This led the Greens to ask an additional question that went beyond the scope of their family: "So what are we doing with the resources God has provided to present Christ to as many people as possible?" As a family, they agreed on several truths. Life is like a vapor; it passes away all too quickly. Temporal things don't last. Institutions rise and fall. Only the eternal things endure. Therefore, they believe the more they give to God's work, the bigger impact they could have eternally. David said,

> God created our family to affect as many people as possible with eternal life by letting them know about the greatest gift ever given. How can we not share the greatest gift ever with others? So, I ask God, "What else can we do to save one more person for eternity?" There is always something else we can do to save one more soul. We can't rest as long as there is one more.

One more. David references Oskar Schindler in the closing scene of Steven Spielberg's movie, *Schindler's List*. Even though his courageous efforts saved over 1,100 Jews, Oskar was tormented and lamented, "I didn't do enough! I could have gotten more out. I could have gotten one more person—and I didn't."

One more. That is what drives David Green and his family.

***

Once the kid who froze when asked to give an oral report in high school, David overcame his fears, called on God's strength, and started accepting speaking requests on a limited basis. Today, he is a highly sought-after speaker and has capped at six or seven the number of speaking engagements he will prayerfully accept each year.

David has humbly received the Ernst and Young LLP National Entrepreneur of the Year award, the Primedia Award of Excellence as the Chain Store of the Year in 1997, an honorary doctorate degree in Business Management from Indiana Wesleyan University, the Christian Business Men's Connection Salt and Light Award in 2006, Arizona Christian University's Daniel Award for Courageous Public Faith, and the Zig Ziglar Servant Leadership award in 2015.

What will the future bring? David is committed to improving constantly and growing the Hobby Lobby tree instead of starting new, unrelated businesses. He hopes to double the size and therefore the fruit available for giving in the next decade. Other than that, no family member is willing to predict what will come. Steve said,

> Whatever I can think of probably won't happen. Who could have ever predicted that we would be involved in a Supreme Court case over sanctity of life and religious liberty?

David has a different desk today. He occasionally crawls under it, too; but now, he does it to praise God, recall all that

God has done for him and his family, and contemplate how he can love and honor God as prescribed in the proverb he has made his daily commitment:

> Trust in the Lord with all your heart and lean not on your own understanding; in all your ways submit to him, and he will make your paths straight. (Proverbs 3:5-6)

(Author's note: Excerpts from David Green's book, More Than a Hobby, have been integrated into this chapter. I highly recommend David's book, as well as his latest book released in 2017, Giving It All Away and Getting It Back Again. You will find them fascinating and informative.)

Personal Reflection and Group Discussion

1. David stated that he became prideful in his early success and, as a result, made himself too big and God too small. He was relying on his own instincts and resources and not enough on seeking and trusting God's will and guidance. Do you need to let God get bigger in your life? If so, how? How does Proverbs 3:5 and its declaration speak to you?

2. What is your core business that best aligns with your God-given unique abilities? Is growing this core your primary focus?

3. Can you improve your company's unity around purpose? Unity around process? Unity fostered by leadership? Unity around accountability? How will you do so?

4. When it comes to combining business economics and honoring God, David shared, "You can't always get there with a calculator." What business decisions have you made where you chose to honor God even though they didn't seem to make economic business sense? What was the result?

5. Have you ever taken a risk or made a major decision without first consulting God? How do you believe that decision could've turned out differently with God's guidance?

6. What other spiritual, business, and personal concepts and practices noted in this chapter stood out to you? How will you integrate them into your life and/or business?

WHY NOT?

THE LATE LARRY BURKETT, founder of Crown Financial Ministries who is referenced by Alan Sears in the Foreword to this book, wrote the classic bestseller, *Business by the Book*. As Larry's successor at Crown, I have had the privilege of meeting thousands of entrepreneurs and business leaders across the world who have faithfully adopted his charge to operate their businesses with excellence for the glory of God. Countless business leaders have acted in obedience to God's Word to form the basis of the purpose and operation of their enterprise with outstanding results. I have always desired to see some of the profound practical and spiritual differences these businesses have made in the world chronicled in a case study format for others to learn from. Certainly, not all of these stories can be credited to Larry's work, but Jeff Holler has written a book close to my heart: case studies of those who have built their business "by the Book."

Jeff has taken us on a tour around the world to meet some of God's choice leaders—and what a tour it has been! Through his capable interviewing and writing skills, we have had the rare privilege of a close-up, transparent, and personal look into the lives of contemporary entrepreneurs who are motivated by a purpose *Bigger Than Business*. These are men and women who have built an enterprise forged from hearts that have been fully surrendered to the Master, and their impact is beyond inspiring.

From Dallas, Texas, we met Michael and Debbie Rasa, whose lives were battered by self-inflicted pain followed by heartache and suffering. They lived by the philosophy of this world to "work hard and play hard" and found themselves empty and being torn apart despite their business success. Out of the ashes, God took control and rewrote their story into one of meaning, purpose, and beauty. They now transparently share the story of their rescue and redemption. They pour into their staff and employees and work to advance God's kingdom, not their own.

Have you invited God to rescue you from your sin and to redeem you from your mistakes? Have you asked Him to make beauty out of your ashes?

From the Sunshine Coast of Australia, we met Dr. Robi Sonderegger, whose unique entrepreneurial bent and tireless work ethic, both inherited from his father, led him to pursue a career in psychology. By going through a series of what he called "sliding door" moments, Dr. Robi found his wife, his faith, and his passion to help those mentally and emotionally devastated by trauma. Today, his innovative programs are helping churches, faith-based groups, and mental health professionals worldwide bring hope to the hurting.

Have you, like Dr. Robi, pledged to trust God completely and follow wherever He leads, knowing His plan is bigger and better than you could ever conceive? Do you avoid or step through the "sliding doors" moments God places in your path?

From Pompeia, Brazil, we met Jorge Nishimura, whose remarkable journey to lead one of the nation's greatest family-owned businesses reads like the story of Joseph who extended grace to the very brothers who once discarded him as worthless. We learned of the deeply held values that guide the company and its commitment to *bumpuku*, that happiness is found in sharing. Their life purpose is not to accumulate things but to serve others for God's glory. Their generosity has touched millions of lives in the nation where their late father once immigrated as a pauper.

Have you forgiven those who have wronged you in your family or business? Have you identified the deeply held values that will guide your company to a purpose greater than accumulating more and more money?

From Memphis, Tennessee, we met Alan and Katherine Barnhart, whose plans to serve as missionaries in the Middle East were redirected by God to make the then-small family business, Barnhart Crane and Rigging, their primary basis for service. Through excellent practices and strong principled growth, today, the family business now gives an astonishing $1.5 million per month to advance the expansion of God's kingdom. Alan and Katherine don't believe there are "Christian companies," just Christians working in companies guided by biblical principles. They are not content at their current level of giving but are striving to do more to serve God through their work and generosity.

Are you operating your business by biblical financial principles? Are you striving to do more to serve God and give more for His glory?

From Kigali, Rwanda, we met Grace Nyirabarinda and the inspirational Amarhoro sewing ladies. Their business produces quality products and earns modest profits for themselves but also serves other hurting families in their community where they make loans while demonstrating mercy and kindness in a nation once torn apart by unspeakable violence. They have chosen to be forgivers and reconcilers, not victims. They are committed to healing hearts.

Are you using your business to help the hurting? Are you a forgiver? Can your company inspire the least in your community and set an example of kindness to all you serve?

From Jakarta, Indonesia, we met Dr. Suparno Adijanto, who is motivated to clear the path for others because he gratefully acknowledges that God and others have done the same for him. As the leader of a large public company based in a majority Muslim nation, Suparno operates with core Christian values of stewardship, community, partnership, and commitment. In all his business and volunteer roles, he has a clear purpose to point others to the excellency of Christ.

Are you clearing the path for others? Are you giving back in proportion to what God and others have done for you? Are you setting an example of the excellency of Christ in your business and service?

From Saxony, Germany, we met Frank Suchy, who was raised in communist East Germany and was comfortably settled into his government-approved work as a mechanic for textile machinery when his career and life took a dramatic turn. Through both the woman who became his wife and a caring pastor, Frank became a Christian. As he realized his faith conflicted with totalitarianism, he set out on a risky, daring journey that led to the founding of his own company and the opportunity to positively influence Christian business organizations throughout Europe, even as the walls of communism fell. Today, he has added a publishing business to support entrepreneurs and business leaders to find their calling from God for their lives.

Has your faith in God prompted you to take professional risk in pursuit of honoring Him? How can you broaden your influence and impact on other Christian business leaders?

Finally, from Oklahoma City, Oklahoma, we met David Green and learned the "rest of the story" of how Hobby Lobby and Green Family Enterprises were guided step by step by an absolute, unwavering faith in God as they grew to become one of America's most influential Christian-led companies. We met a humble servant driven by the desire to reach "just one more" with the gospel that has guided his every decision to grow his company and to obey God with bold choices such as to close on Sundays and to challenge a government law that threatened the religious freedoms of all Christian business owners. We learned the real "why" that drives their purpose, which goes far beyond growing a business for personal gain.

Have you defined your purpose for operating your business beyond growing the bottom line? Have you committed to making bold decisions in obedience to God's direction, no matter the consequences you may face?

Jeff has helped us to see clearly the *why*. We have met those who are doing business by the book. It is time to respond to the challenge of adopting a purpose *Bigger Than Business*.

Why not you?

Why not now?

CHUCK BENTLEY
CEO, Crown Financial Ministries
Knoxville, Tennessee

CONCLUDING QUESTIONS

1. Someone once said, "You can't know God's will if you don't know God's Word." Even though they are some of the busiest people on the planet, all the people featured in this book obtain great wisdom, direction, and joy through regularly reading and contemplating God's biblical truths. They make the time, and their return on investment (ROI) of this time is life-changing. What can you do to increase your understanding and contemplation of God's Word as it applies to your life and purpose? Do you regularly participate in formal Bible studies? Do you, at a minimum, have a habit of doing a daily devotional?

2. What does the call to be a good and faithful servant mean to you? Have your thoughts on this subject changed in any manner after reading the stories shared in this book? How will you answer the call?

3. When you strip away everything else, what are your motives for doing what you do in and through your business? What does your time allocation and use of your discretionary income say about your motives? From a financial perspective, do you honor the biblical mandate to give back to God a minimum of 10 percent of your first fruits (including 10 percent of your profit)? If not, why not? If yes, should you give more?

4. How do those with whom you work and interact understand and experience your faith? Do they know the source of your values and what is at the core of your humility and faithful living?

5. Several of the people featured in this book found financial freedom and flexibility by following the biblical principle of limited use of debt. What will it do for you and your business if you dramatically reduce your debt? Are you willing to invest the time to create a plan to do so?

6. Every one of the book's personalities and their company associates have put an immense amount of time into finding ways to get the right people in the right jobs; building supporting leadership, management, and accountability structures; developing the processes, tools, and technology necessary to make the processes dependable, repeatable, and efficient; and to always be thinking ahead about what they need to do next to accomplish their mission. What business leadership and management insights in the book were most compelling to you? List them, and then ask those best suited to help to assist you in prioritizing and planning how you will improve these functions in your company.

ENDNOTES

[1] Joseph Astrachan, Ph.D., editor, Family Business Review,
  http://www.fbagr.org/index.php?option=com_content&view=articl
  e&id=117&Itemid=75

[2] Liz Essley Whtye, "Giving It All," Philanthropy Magazine, Spring
  2014.

[3] www.hobbylobby.com/site3/ministry/message.cfm

ACKNOWLEDGEMENTS

FIRST, I GIVE IMMEASURABLE GRATITUDE to my Father in Heaven for leading me to each of the subjects and for inspiring me with the words to convey their stories and hearts.

Words are insufficient to describe the fullness of my appreciation for the book's subjects: Dr. Suparno Adijanto, Alan Barnhart, David Green, Jorge Nishimura, Grace Nyirabarinda, Michael and Debbie Rasa, Dr. Robi Sonderegger, and Frank Suchy. Thank you for your valuable time invested with me, for sharing your amazing stories, and for the incredible kingdom-building difference you are making by seeking and following God's will and purpose for your lives.

I also thank all of those who God placed in my life who have helped me to experience the joy of relationship. Some have already passed before me—like my beloved mom and dad—and many are those with whom I interact regularly, including my remarkable family and my cherished friends. You should know that I thank God for you every day, and I believe I am one of the most blessed men on the planet because of you!

My wife, Charlsey, understood from the beginning that it was not my idea to write a book but rather saw the hand of God leading me to do so. She knew that the many wonderful relationships to which God has led me over the years were on purpose, and comprehended that God had something bigger in play than business or friendships. She saw me struggling to manage the research, interviews, notes summarizations, additional research, and writing of this book. At a critical juncture, Charlsey volunteered to join me for three interviews to take notes and then to return home and integrate our handwritten notes with the audio, a major endeavor that cleared the path for me to focus on the writing. Charlsey also helped to review and edit each chapter and provided inspired insight. Charlsey, I am forever grateful when you believe in me—no matter the unexpected direction or kind of endeavor that God's path takes us—and for your support and encouragement. You have given purpose to me from the day I met you.

Our daughters, Stacy and Jennifer, are two of my greatest blessings and were kind enough not to have me committed when I announced that it was prayerfully clear to me that God wanted me to write this book. Never doubting my abilities (so she said), Jennifer nevertheless sent a book to me on how to write a book, which was actually very helpful. Thank you both for being such wonderful daughters and for adding immeasurable depth and beauty to my purpose. Your prayers and encouragement are infinitely appreciated.

While writing, I missed too many of my grandchildren's soccer games and activities. Thank you, Papa's Buddy, Papa's Little Darling, Papa's Little Sweetheart, Papa's Little Chief, and Papa's Little Sweet P (aka. Papa's Team) for understanding and for loving me so fully and sweetly. Your hugs and kisses are the best! I am so very proud of you and love you bigger than Texas!

My dear friend, Alan Sears, whom I admire immensely, initially suggested and then urged me to write this book. I jokingly tell Alan that I will forgive him—someday. In hindsight, I realize Alan is probably the only person on the planet who could have gotten me to seriously pray about and consider writing a book. Thank you, Alan, for being such a fabulous vessel for God and His work, and thank you for your friendship, encouragement, and extremely valued ongoing assistance.

God placed in my life the right people at exactly the right times for this book to become a reality.

Angela Walthall, The Capital Chart Room, LTD Executive Support Manager, worked miracles with my schedule to provide me the time to complete the book while not allowing The Capital Chart Room, LTD and our client work to miss a beat. Thank you also for your great research, review, and editing work on the book. I am also grateful to the entire Capital Chart Room, LTD team for taking such great care of our clients! I am also grateful to Tammy Sheppard, The Capital Chart Room, LTD Administrative Assistant, who volunteered to transcribe the audio for the final two interviews when Charlsey had to divert her time to help a family member with a medical issue. Thank you for the much-needed assist.

Dale and Judy Dawson and Dub Stocker—thank you for inviting me (without prior approval) to Crown Financial Ministry's Christian Economic Forum where I met its leader and CEO, Chuck Bentley. Thank you, Dale, for also leading me to Peter King, who led me to Peter Janssen, both of whom helped me in Australia.

Chuck Bentley, as you are in God's kingdom, you were a difference maker for me and this book. You took the time to get to the heart of what I wanted to convey and then introduced me to Jorge Nishimura, Dr. Suparno Adijanto, and Alan Barnhart, whose stories were a perfect fit for the book. And, it was through your Christian Economic Forum that I met Dr. Robi Sonderegger, and also Timo Plutschinski, who introduced me to Frank Suchy. (Thank you, Timo.) You have continued to encourage and help me with your valuable insight and advice. Most valued, however, is your love and friendship and that of your family. Thank you!

J.D. Hall, thank you for your interest in me and the book, and as a result, for your introduction to Michael and Debbie Rasa. There is good reason why your parents and their friends are so proud of you, including Charlsey and me.

Thanks to Larry Rybka for leading Charlsey and me to Rwanda, Africa, and together with Heidi Morgan, for introducing us to the Arise Rwanda Ministries, Bridge2Rwanda Ministries, and to the Amahoro sewing ladies. Larry, your friendship, example, wisdom, and kingdom-building business and personal endeavors have made a positive impact on innumerable lives, including mine! Thank you also, Heidi, for your Christ-like care for us while in Rwanda and for your friendship.

Brother John Gasangwa, thank you, my friend, for being the translator for my interview with Grace and the Amahoro sewing ladies and for your incredible example of obedience to God's will for your life, keeping your promises to God, and what it means to trust God with all your heart!

Thanks to Joan C. Webb for throwing me a lifeline exactly when I needed it by providing me the insight and tools necessary to complete the book, find the right editor, and begin working on publishing.

Adam Colwell, you are the right editor to whom Joan introduced me. We couldn't have worked together any better. I appreciate you personally, your patience with me, your thorough process, and your outstanding work. Thank you, my friend!

Darren Shearer, my publisher, was introduced to me by one of the endorsers of the book. He told me beforehand that he felt Darren and his company, High Bridge Books, were a perfect fit for me. He was right! Thank you, Darren, for patiently guiding Adam and I through the publishing and marketing process.

TO GOD BE THE GLORY!

GO 'NOLES